'There are many books about motivation and they tend to rely on pop psychology or the author's intuition, which makes them as inaccurate as ineffective. With *Get Things Done*, Robert Kelsey has managed to bridge the gap between the science and practice of willpower, discussing key psychological theories in an elegant, accessible style, and translating them into effective actionable suggestions. This book is a must-read for anybody wishing to understand the difference between potential and achievement, and wanting to bridge that gap to fulfil their meaningful goals.'

**Tomas Chamorro-Premuzic, PhD, author of *Confidence: Overcoming Low Self-esteem, Insecurity and Self-doubt***

'A great contribution for all of us who struggle with disorder and long to attain meaningful goals. It gives us both the why and the how!'

**Dr Marilyn Paul, author of *It's Hard to Make a Difference When You Can't Find Your Keys***

'A Smörgåsbord of practical tips for getting your life under control.'

**John Williams, author of *Screw Work Let's Play***

'An engaging, entertaining, easy-to-read book. Robert Kelsey is disarmingly honest about his own flaws and failings and you can really hear his voice in his writing. If you're looking to make a journey of personal change, you could do worse than to rely on Kelsey as your compass.'

**Dr Rob Yeung, psychologist at consulting firm Talentspace and author of *Confidence* and *How to Win***

'The hallmarks of Robert Kelsey's work are thorough research, personal insight and thoughtful presentation.'

**John Caunt, author of *Organise Yourself***

W0113609

'The world is full of dreamers; talented individuals with great abilities, ideas and aspirations. And yet, many of these dreamers fail to realize their full potential. How sad is that? In his book, *Get Things Done*, author Robert Kelsey shares the secrets of making things happen. He tackles both psychological and behavioural blocks, and gives us practical ways to deal with potential distractions such as email, conflict, bad habits, etc. His writing style is genuine, easy to read and based on solid research. I recommend this book for anyone out there who knows they have even more potential than they are currently demonstrating. You want to get results in your life? Then start by reading this book!'

**Tim Ursiny, Ph.D., RCC, CBC, founder of Advantage Coaching & Training and author of multiple books including *The Coward's Guide to Conflict* and *The Top Performer's Guide to Attitude***

'Robert's thought-provoking survey of productivity literature looks at the perplexing question of why smart people can undermine their own success. Fortunately, this book offers plenty of ideas for getting started on the hard work of personal change.'

**Laura Vanderkam, author of *What the Most Successful People Do at Work***

'For those that want to achieve more, working out how to get things done is vital. When it comes to understanding how to turn yourself into a doer this book is a great kick in the pants.'

**Richard Newton, co-author of *Stop Talking, Start Doing***

'Finding fulfilling work takes endeavour. It also takes direction and motivation. Robert Kelsey's well-researched book is a great place to start.'

**Roman Krznaric, bestselling author of *How to Find Fulfilling Work***

# Get Things Done

## What Stops Smart People Achieving More and How You Can Change

Robert Kelsey

CAPSTONE
A Wiley Brand

© 2014 What's Stopping You Ltd

What's Stopping You? is a trademark of What's Stopping You Ltd

*Registered office*

John Wiley and Sons Ltd, The Atrium, Southern Gate, Chichester, West Sussex, PO19 8SQ, United Kingdom

For details of our global editorial offices, for customer services and for information about how to apply for permission to reuse the copyright material in this book please see our website at www.wiley.com.

The right of the author to be identified as the author of this work has been asserted in accordance with the Copyright, Designs and Patents Act 1988.

All rights reserved. No part of this publication may be reproduced, stored in a retrieval system, or transmitted, in any form or by any means, electronic, mechanical, photocopying, recording or otherwise, except as permitted by the UK Copyright, Designs and Patents Act 1988, without the prior permission of the publisher.

Wiley publishes in a variety of print and electronic formats and by print-on-demand. Some material included with standard print versions of this book may not be included in e-books or in print-on-demand. If this book refers to media such as a CD or DVD that is not included in the version you purchased, you may download this material at http://booksupport.wiley.com. For more information about Wiley products, visit www.wiley.com.

Designations used by companies to distinguish their products are often claimed as trademarks. All brand names and product names used in this book and on its cover are trade names, service marks, trademark or registered trademarks of their respective owners. The publisher and the book are not associated with any product or vendor mentioned in this book. None of the companies referenced within the book have endorsed the book.

Limit of Liability/Disclaimer of Warranty: While the publisher and author have used their best efforts in preparing this book, they make no representations or warranties with the respect to the accuracy or completeness of the contents of this book and specifically disclaim any implied warranties of merchantability or fitness for a particular purpose. It is sold on the understanding that the publisher is not engaged in rendering professional services and neither the publisher nor the author shall be liable for damages arising herefrom. If professional advice or other expert assistance is required, the services of a competent professional should be sought.

*Library of Congress Cataloging-in-Publication Data is available*

A catalogue record for this book is available from the British Library.

ISBN 978–0-857–08308–1 (paperback) ISBN 978–0-857–08322–7 (ebk)

ISBN 978–0-857–08321–0 (ebk)

Cover design by Simon Dovar

Set in 10/13.5 pt Sabon LT Std by Toppan Best-set Premedia Limited

Printed in Great Britain by TJ International Ltd, Padstow, Cornwall, UK

*To my mother*

# CONTENTS

# INTRODUCTION

# MY OWN PERSONAL CHAOS

In my mid-twenties I started learning German. Not sure why. I just fancied it – perhaps feeling that, having earned a university degree (late), I could plug another 'life gap' and learn a language. I went to the *Goethe-Institut* in Manchester and borrowed some tapes. And I made good progress. Soon I felt well on my way – building up vocabulary, understanding verb construction and dealing with grammar.

But then I just stopped. One day I missed a lesson and that was that. Of course, 20 years have passed, so if I'd kept it up I'd be fluent by now.

In my early thirties I took up sailing. I was living in New York at the time and had some great lessons in the harbour using Liberty and Ellis Island as tacking points. And I was good at it – my instructor thought me a 'natural'. But, again, I just stopped – meaning my strong nautical progress came to nothing.

Then there was golf – that was in my early twenties. French – early thirties. Five-a-side football, squash, tennis – all sometime between university and now. And what about all those business plans? Town-based restaurant guides, for instance. We produced three but not a fourth despite their popularity. A highly-focused financial magazine: didn't happen, despite two near-identical magazines since succeeding. A lifestyle magazine for the City of London: yep, there's one of those now. But it's nothing to do with me.

And the books I've half written. There was *The War Hero*, a Second World War tale of a discharged soldier lying about the circumstances of his injury; an unnamed spy novel based in a fictional country; a romantic drama called *Sanctuary* involving a Manchester student and a young Asian girl running away from a forced marriage; and even a lad-lit comedy called *Mind The Gap* on finding love in London. In each case I made strong progress – writing reams and reams. And then I simply stopped.

Yet such frivolities seem insignificant compared to my wayward career path. Enough to raise eyebrows in any HR department, my serious 'careers' have included training as a building surveyor (four years, plus a year at poly), work as an advertising sales executive (one year), a newspaper production editor/journo (one year), a magazine sub-editor (six months), a financial journalist (five years), an investment banker (five years), a dotcom entrepreneur (two years) and a financial PR company director (ten years). In fact, anyone trying to make sense of my CV would assume they'd picked up a page or two from the pile below.

## Process isn't a talent – it's taught

Just about everything in my life has followed the same wayward trajectory: bright ideas, followed by enthusiasm, followed by an active frenzy that fizzles out once the going gets tough or I become bored or something else attracts my attention. Despite looking and acting well-organized – and possessing plenty of early determination – my mental chaos ultimately wins: halting progress and destroying both my productivity and my credibility. The only alternative to this pattern has been when fear has overwhelmed even this pathetic process – stopping me from even starting.

That said, I'm far from alone. Millions of people are stymied by their inability to get things done. They cannot get beyond the idea or initial thought – or perhaps the half-page of scribbled lines. Even if they take action they can fall at the first fence, or the minute another – seemingly better – idea takes its place. Many eventually surrender – assuming it takes skills beyond them; or that those that can get things done have innate gifts they'll never acquire.

Of course, they don't. They've simply learnt the art (and science) of process. Indeed, process is a key word. As described within, there are conditions aplenty to explain our inability to deal with process. Yet there's also the fact that process is a skill we need to acquire, like learning to read a book from the beginning to the end (i.e. in that order). That said, millions of people enter adulthood without learning the basics of process. For me, the concept of thinking before acting – and then acting with thought given to sequence (and consequence) – was alien.

The problem wasn't just impulsivity. Sure, I'd often jump in without thought, although I'd just as often not jump at all (perhaps when facing authority or bureaucracy or when feeling fearful or lazy). My problem was being clueless with respect to time and task management, which meant my actions had no direction or purpose, while instructions felt like an imposition: hence my knee-jerk resistance.

As we shall see, such cluelessness starts young and is almost certainly the result of poor conditioning: whether from influencers (such as parents and teachers) who were themselves poorly conditioned (thus merely passing on the malaise), or who we – for whatever reason – ignored or even rejected.

And it's not long before we become resigned to our fate: developing low expectations regarding what's achievable, or assuming that – somehow – strong goal-oriented productivity is for other people. We may even find a condition that suits our symptoms, perhaps excusing us from the fray (see Part One).

Yet there's nothing innate about strong personal productivity. In virtually all circumstances it's a mere facet of learning. It's something we have to be taught, or something we have to teach ourselves if no one bothered (or we didn't listen). Blaming others or our circumstances, or assuming others have privileges and entitlements not available to us, is both disabling and self-fulfilling.

Of course, we're right: other people *are* (probably) to blame for our situation; and others *do* have it easier. And we may even have been diagnosed with one of the long list of conditions to explain our productive deficiencies. But using this as an excuse to languish at the bottom – to not even start the journey towards becoming a well-organized, goal-oriented and productive human being – is an appalling and wilful act of self-sabotage.

Someone, somewhere has to tell us this news. And (more importantly) we have to hear it. Otherwise, like millions of unproductive people everywhere, we'll remain stuck in the wrong place – facing the wrong way – although with some cast-iron excuses for our lack of progress.

## Someone capable of achieving something

No mentor appeared for me – at least not one I was willing to listen to. Instead, I remained utterly ineffective until my late thirties. Of course, I did make *some* headway. But it was poor progress compared to what I thought possible, and usually dismissed by me as 'too little, too late'. Somewhere in there, I reasoned, was a person able to achieve great things. I just needed someone to spot it, give me a chance, and point me in the right direction.

But that moment never came. In fact, even by thinking this, I'd handed over my future to somebody I'd never met and who possibly did not exist – hence my starry-eyed 'gis-a-job' look of longing and desperation every time I met somebody that clearly did have a future, and did know where they were going.

How pathetic: inwardly pleading 'save me' to total strangers, asking them (even if unstated, the intent was plain) to rescue me by organizing my future. It was the directionless graduate's equivalent of sitting passively outside the train station with a sign saying 'homeless and hungry'.

Yet the biggest problem with this 'future-outsourcing' approach isn't that it doesn't work. It's that it does. Occasionally, we do get rescued – normally by someone looking for recruits to their cause. We end up pursuing *their* goals for *their* ends. Indeed, why not? We've failed to forge our own path, so we may as well hand over our fate to someone more capable. That said, we'll quickly blame them when our unrealistic expectations turn out to be, well, unrealistic.

## Ever-decreasing circles

On several occasions I've outsourced the direction of my career in this way: pleading for a chance (covertly if not overtly) and 'as luck would have it' being recruited by an organized, goal-oriented, skipper looking for a crew. Eventually I'd work this out and become disillusioned and even resentful. And then I'd start the same flirty-eyed process all over again, with a new bunch of productive strangers.

As is the way with these things, this was a process that repeated itself in ever-decreasing circles until – depressed and not a little fearful for the future – the unrelenting reality of my situation came crashing in. Floored, I found the self-help section of the bookshop – a zone that opened up an Aladdin's cave of potential solutions for my malaise. Books, DVDs, courses, even homeopathic remedies: rather typically I jumped in with the zeal of those desperate to be converted.

But, again, I'd outsourced my future – this time to a series of grinning Californians promising me dream-fulfilment via their seemingly irrefutable methodologies. Not for the first time, my wide-eyed enthusiasm became eroded by small slips and minor setbacks. My passion burnt away – replaced by a deep cynicism at the cheesy grins, the hyper-titling (*Maximum Achievement*, *Unlimited Power* etc.) and the over-promising.

That said, the pattern of behaviour felt uniquely mine. Hope, enthusiasm, sketched plans, erratic execution, small setbacks, arrested progress, despondent reactions, procrastination, surrender, cynicism, denial, even depression – and then, almost without pause, the next twinkling light on the horizon rekindling the hope.

## Lost in a fantasy world

In fact, mine is a simple tale of low self-esteem and childhood alienation: a strained relationship with my father; a school that only noticed my misbehaviour; an older sister that I seemed to continually irritate; and a mother who tried to make up for all these deficits while busy fighting her own battles. Small wonder that formalized pursuits couldn't hold my attention and, instead, I lost myself in a fantasy world that, after a while, consumed my sense of purpose.

I opted out of the real, emotionally painful world at the age of ten – instead occupying a parallel, more comforting universe of my own making. Literally, I became someone else – a made-up person in a made-up country – keen to escape the reality of an upbringing that was both barren and hurtful.

I was brought up in what Americans call exurbia – a once-quaint Essex village expanded to the size of a small town to house the post-war east London diaspora in soulless but comfortable estates. This changed the pace of life along with the accents. Yet neither the rural natives, with their fruity vowels, nor the London incomers, with their sharp expressions, offered me a sense of direction worth emulating. Instead, I left the local comprehensive with one O level (in geography) and pursued a series of careers I didn't want. Or, with those I did want, eventually rebelled against – perhaps after an episode in which I felt exploited or undervalued.

A crucial point here is that unproductive people are rarely lazy – at least not initially. They can be highly motivated and work extremely hard, although they're busy going nowhere. Add stress, anxiety and convictions of exploitation to those patent feelings of frustration and alienation and this is a destructive state of mind. It's also one unlikely to produce a positive response from others.

Most back away: inwardly rolling their eyes or quietly bitching to a confidant. Instead, they focus on their own productive pursuits, and view us as no more than a highly-volatile obstacle to navigate.

## The painful truth

Certainly this cycle continued for me until I went into business with a successful friend – yet again, hitching myself to someone else's endeavours in the hope that some of his magic would rub off. Inevitably, we fell out. But, rather than back away, my partner attacked – telling me some home truths I'd been waiting to hear all my life.

'Yes, you're talented', he said (after prompting). 'But it's wasted. You'll never cash it in because it's directionless. You only know what you don't want, which means you're so busy fighting everybody – including yourself – you become someone others avoid. There's so much noise going on inside your head – so many battles being fought – that you cannot hear or see anything else.'

'In the end, people will give up on you', he said. 'Or you'll spend your entire life running away from things – meaning you'll have nothing to show for it but a series of lost battles and great excuses.'

Finally, someone worth listening to had said something I needed to hear. I had to change, and change fundamentally, which led me back to those discarded self-help books and even into the hands of a professional psychologist.

Yet to change I needed to understand what had happened. Why was I so directionless – destructively so? Adopting productive behaviours simply because some self-help guru told me to – or because a colleague had finally pierced my emotional armour – felt equally unsustainable: another pursuit that would disappear at the first sign of boredom, or after the first setback, or due to some invented dispute.

If I was to change fundamentally – sustainably – I first had to unravel the chaotic mind that made me so ineffectual. Only then could I adopt the strong habits – as recommended by the gurus – with any sense of understanding, or with any optimism that the road ahead would be more rewarding than the twisting and rutted path that had taken me to this sorry point.

**Get Things Done:** *Whatever the cause, many people spend their lives in a cycle of hope, enthusiasm and endeavour followed by setbacks, defeat and cynicism. The result is procrastination, low attainment and frustrated ambitions. To break this cycle we need to unravel our chaotic minds.*

# PART ONE

# The Unproductive Mind

# 1

# ORGANIZATIONAL INCOMPETENCE

Nestled in the gentle hills of California's Silicon Valley sits Stanford University: the breeding ground for the area's innovators since a horse-stud farm was converted into the original campus in 1891. Yet this university is renowned for more than being the intellectual hub of the most innovative community in the world's leading technological nation. In the 1960s and early 1970s Stanford University became known as a major centre for psychology – and particularly for a series of ground-breaking experiments on children that were to shape thinking on motivation, drive and success.

And while many of the experiments have been forgotten by all but a select group of professionals, one has entered the realms of folklore: the 1972 marshmallow tests on impulse control.

Brought into a room and given a single marshmallow, a succession of four-year-old children were then offered a choice: eat the marshmallow now, or resist for 15 minutes and receive a second marshmallow as a reward. Unbeknown to them, this simple choice – dividing the children into those that managed to wait for the additional marshmallow and those that didn't – revealed a fissure that would potentially run right through their lives, according to the psychologists at Stanford (led by Walter Mischel). This was between those able to *defer gratification* – and therefore develop productive, future-oriented organizational competence – and those preferring impulse-driven *instant gratification*, who were thus condemned to organizational incompetence and underachievement.

These were not stupid kids. They were mostly the offspring of campus professionals or graduates, so were likely to be destined for strong educational attainment. Yet, when tracked down and interviewed in adolescence, they again fell into two camps that corresponded closely with the results of the earlier experiments. Those capable of resisting the single marshmallow at four were more likely to be optimistic, competent, self-reliant and trustworthy. They were confident teenagers with strong initiative and clear goals. Yet those who'd been unable to resist the marshmallow were more troubled: revealing traits such as pessimism, impulsiveness, envy, mistrust, anger, resentment and indecision.

Basically, one group – the marshmallow resisters – expected and were organized for success; while the other group – the marshmallow eaters – were not.

'There is perhaps no psychological skill more fundamental than resisting impulse', writes Daniel Goleman in *Emotional Intelligence* (1995), one of the many books to cite these famous experiments. 'It is the root of all self-control, since all emotions, by their very nature, lead to one or another impulse to act.'

Delayed or deferred gratification is, therefore, a key trait in productive competence. Those lacking willpower or self-control will seek instant gratification, states Goleman, whether through sought pleasure or avoided pain. While those with self-control will ignore short-term inconveniences and temptations in order to focus on future potential rewards.

## Early-life conditioning

Of course, everyone who's ever read about the marshmallow test immediately wonders how they'd have reacted to such temptation as a four-year-old child. The truth is, we cannot know; although I had that uneasy feeling of recognition – suspecting I'd have been incapable of delayed gratification.

Yet my feelings of unease extended to the marshmallow test itself. As a four-year-old, my guess is I'd have misunderstood the terms of the offer. So focused would I have been on the treat in front of me, I'd have filtered out any other information, including the potential for reward if I waited for the adult to return. Did this, therefore, condemn me at four as innately incapable of deferring gratification? Or did it simply suggest it was something I'd yet to learn?

This left me wondering whether there was anything hardwired (or even genetic) being measured by the marshmallow test, as some of those commenting on the Stanford experiments suggest. Or could early-life conditioning be dictating the result – encouraging the obvious follow-on that, unless this conditioning is reversed or amended at some point on our route towards adulthood, we'll reveal the same traits throughout our lives?

So, while I was convinced I'd have failed the marshmallow test at four – and probably even at eight – I was far from convinced this meant I was innately disposed (potentially genetically) towards unproductive, impulse-driven behaviour. It was simply poor, yet reversible, conditioning.

## Testing the marshmallow test

To test this I did my own, totally unscientific, experiment on four children I knew well: my own and those of a friend and neighbour. Left together (although the Stanford children were alone I wanted to observe the impact of influence on the children) – each with a single marshmallow – I secretly watched the reactions of boys aged three, four and six and a girl who'd turned seven that day.

Despite the distractions of the occasion, the seven-year-old immediately understood my promise to return with an additional marshmallow if the original remained uneaten. She held on the required 15 minutes, which was no more than I expected from this emotionally aware young girl.

And her good behaviour influenced the six-year-old boy. That said, he seemed able to wait only by creating a game that mimicked the movements of the girl: with them alternating between sitting on their hands and clasping their hands over their mouths. I suspect he'd have found it a lot harder without her good example – especially as he talked constantly about the reward, as well as how long my return was taking.

The younger two had a far tougher time, however. The three-year-old lasted less than a minute, although I became convinced he only understood the premise after realizing the cost of his action: as excitedly reminded by his elders. This distressed him to the point he had to be removed from the room to avoid disrupting the experiment entirely.

Meanwhile, the four-year-old hung on, although was constantly asking his sister for an explanation and was clearly troubled by the challenge. Only the verbal intervention of the older boy (a strong influencer of the younger boy's behaviour) prevented him gobbling the marshmallow at around the five-minute mark and then repeatedly from around minute eight. Again, I worried throughout that he'd misunderstood the proposition.

## Delayed gratification is developmental

Of course, my own version of the experiment proves nothing, although I thought the exact matching of the children's age to their ability to resist was surely no coincidence – meaning that delayed gratification is as likely developmental as it is innate. It's something we learn. As for the Stanford marshmallow failures and their negative traits in young adulthood, could the same poor conditioning that prevented them developing strong productive behaviour at four last right into young adulthood?

In fact, it could last a lifetime. A 2011 follow-up study – conducted by Dr B.J. Casey of Weill Cornell Medical College in New York – noticed that those adept at delayed gratification in the original Stanford test revealed similarly enabling traits as they approached middle-age. As for the instant-gratifiers in 1972, they too revealed similarly disabling propensities in the most recent study. And worryingly (at least for those assuming conditioning the central issue), the 2011 experiments recorded brain-pattern correlations suggesting the existence of a 'seat of self-control' (or otherwise) in the prefrontal cortex of the brain.

Yet Casey's experiments sampled just 59 out of the original 600 tested at Stanford. And these were the most extreme cases (at either end of the spectrum) recorded by Mischel in 1972. So a correlation was always a likely outcome. Of more interest – at least for the vast-majority of middling types – would have been a study of those that fell between these two extremes. It is this group – the 540 not retested by Casey – where success or failure would have been most likely due to conditioning.

Indeed, my guess is that many of the 1972 failures would not only now be competent individuals, they'd be able to recall the events that motivated their change from impulsive instant-gratifiers into productive future-oriented professionals. Perhaps, at some point, they became motivated by strong desires or goals (see Part Two). Or maybe they were jolted into productivity via professional training or from starting a new job. Or maybe a new influencer – perhaps from beyond the family – gave them the direction they lacked.

Sure, some will have prospered while others struggled. And those to adopt such competences early will have an advantage. But – given the obvious benefits of delayed gratification and its related traits of productive competence – late adoption is still better than no adoption.

## Freud's id, ego and superego

So we're *not* condemned to a life of impulse-related ineffectiveness at the age of four – an opinion supported by the godfather of psychoanalysis himself. Sigmund Freud's 1920 essay 'Beyond the Pleasure Principle' deals with exactly this issue – later (in a 1923 essay called the 'The Ego and the Id') elaborating his ideas of the 'id', 'ego' and 'superego' to explain the various stages in the development of the human psyche to encompass socialization, planning and organization.

Freud's id contains 'the psychic apparatus at birth' – the instincts to seek pleasure and avoid pain. The id is, according to Freud, 'a cauldron full of seething excitations' that deals with basic needs such as food, water and sex. It's amoral and selfish. It has no sense of time, is completely illogical – primarily sexual – and infantile in its emotional development.

The id is clearly incapable of deferred gratification and needs tempering, although this is something we have to learn (largely from external influences), which is where the ego comes in. The ego acts according to the 'reality principle', says Freud. In contrast to the id's 'pleasure principle', this comprises the organized part of our personality.

'The ego is that part of the id which has been modified by the direct influence of the external world', writes Freud, representing 'what may be called reason and common sense, in contrast to the id, which contains the passions'.

While the ego is only partly conscious, it acts as a restraint on the id – perhaps overriding it with semi-conscious concerns for, say, safety or, importantly, organization. Judgement, tolerance, control, planning, intellect, memory: all are part of Freud's ego.

Guilt, meanwhile, is one of the central characteristics of the superego – the fully-organized part of Freud's personality structure, which acts according to the 'morality principle'. The superego is our conscience – punishing misbehaviour with feelings of guilt. It strives for perfection and is determined to act in a socially appropriate manner – countering the id's need for instant gratification. The superego emerges from learning and brings a sense of personal progress, of future orientation and of integration with social norms.

Given the above descriptions, Freud would have surely viewed a four-year-old child winning a second marshmallow as the early influence of the moderating ego and the organizing superego, most likely due to external guidance. And, importantly, he would have viewed the continuation into early adulthood of traits suggesting an inability to defer gratification as the failure or absence of those same external influences.

For whatever reason, those unable to defer gratification continued to flounder in the id's 'cauldron full of seething excitations'. A cauldron, moreover, that will only lose its appeal once its cost becomes apparent in adulthood: perhaps via wasteful hedonism, addictions, procrastination or an inability to organize for the future.

## Maslow's hierarchy of needs

Yet this leaves one question unanswered. Why would one child develop strong awareness and acceptance of external influences, while another – potentially ignoring or rejecting those same influences – be concerned only with their immediate id-induced stimulation? Of course, this is where some of the marshmallow experimenters suggest an innate propensity for such behaviour, although another famous psychologist offers an alternative explanation.

Abraham Maslow is best known for his 'hierarchy of needs'. First proposed in his 1943 paper 'A Theory of Human Motivation', Maslow's hierarchy is usually expressed as a pyramid – recording a human's development towards what Maslow termed 'self-actualization'.

At the base of the pyramid are basic needs such as air, water and food. Only once these are satisfied can we move to the next level and seek shelter and safety. With these needs met, we seek love and companionship, which – once won – allow us to develop our self-esteem, often via achievement or praise. And once we have

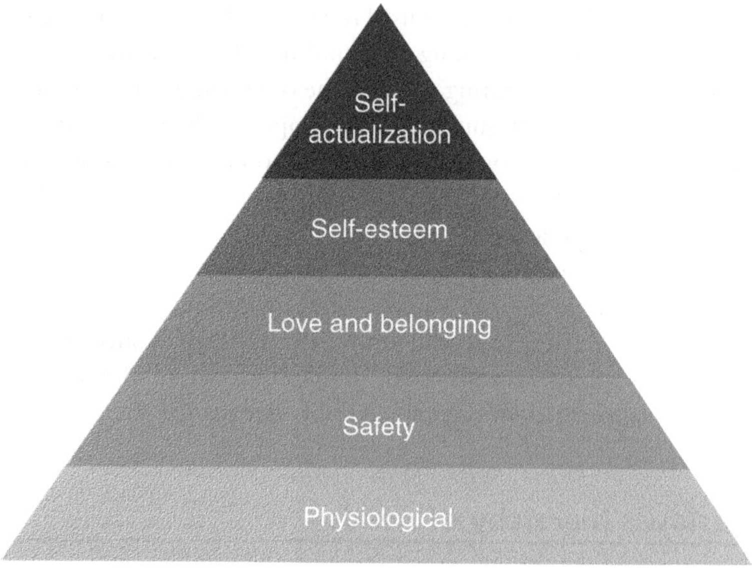


**Figure 1** Maslow's Hierarchy of Needs

self-esteem, we can seek self-actualization, which involves needs such as morality and creativity.

An important point here is that we cannot move to the next level until we have satisfied the needs below. We will not seek shelter without food, or love without safety. Self-esteem, therefore, is impossible without love, meaning we have no motivation towards achievement – and acquiring the productive skills for making progress – unless we first acquire the sense of belonging that comes with love, friendship and acceptance.

Could it be, therefore, that those incapable of deferred gratification at four were revealing early signs of low self-esteem? Lacking the security of love, their impulses were immediate – even basic. And, unless this was actively tackled, such a disablement could stay with them into adulthood.

This certainly had a resonance with me. Having developed low self-esteem as a child – mostly due to feelings of rejection from my father – I felt Maslow's hierarchy explained my erratic tendencies, which lasted well into adulthood.

## Texts that ignore the psychological issues

Yet there's one more aspect to this for those trying to acquire organizational competence in adulthood. It's just possible that the specialist sub-sector of the self-help industry – focusing on time and task management – is of little or no help (at least initially). In fact, it could be viewed as just another distraction, as well as – in the failing – further confirmation of our poor self-beliefs.

Certainly, my response was usually to scan the first chapter of these texts fearful of the emotional and physical investment required to even finish the book, let alone commit to its programme: no wonder they seemed to exacerbate, rather than alleviate, my feelings of low self-worth.

Such books have become a popular genre in recent years. *The Time Trap* by Alec Mackenzie is perhaps the granddaddy. First published in 1972, it adopted the no-nonsense 'take control' approach that has become the accepted style for the majority since. These include *Time Tactics of Very Successful People* by B. Eugene Griessman (1994), *Time Management for Busy People* by Roberta Roesch (1998), *Streetwise Time Management* by Marshall Cook (1999), *Getting Things Done* by David Allen (2001), *Organizing From The Inside Out* by Julie Morgenstern (2004) and *Eat That Frog* by Brian Tracy (2004). Yet there are hundreds of such books.

Although useful – and ransacked for tips and methodologies for the pages ahead – they rarely address the fundamental psychological issues at play with respect to our poor productivity. Nearly all take our organizational inabilities as a starting point and march forward – offering admittedly strong ideas and actions for making the unproductive productive.

Yet this approach assumes we're willing and able to change, as well as capable of putting aside our personal histories in order to take responsibility for our poor productivity. Of course, eventually that's exactly what we have to do. But, first, we must fully understand what led us to this sorry point – something that may take professional psychological help (as it did for me). Only when we comprehend the psychology can we develop strong attributes that convert our destructive and incompetent habits into something more constructive.

**Get Things Done:** *As the marshmallow test demonstrates, delayed gratification is a vital requirement for future-oriented productivity. Yet there's nothing ingrained or genetic being measured. Strong productivity can be learnt. Low self-esteem may lie at the heart of our delayed adoption.*

# 2

# CONDITIONS AND TYPES

Yet there are those claiming our productive or organizational malaise isn't developmental at all. And it's certainly not the result of low self-esteem. Debate rages, but many professionals think the disorganized mind is a diseased mind, and therefore incapable of organizational competence (at least without medical treatment).

Recent decades have seen the 'discovery' of a plethora of illnesses to explain away our productive deficiencies; many – according to their detractors – conforming more to lifestyle trends than hard science.

Attention deficit disorder (ADD or ADHD if including hyperactivity) is probably the best known. A neurobiological condition, ADD is an indication of brain damage or underdevelopment, perhaps to the frontal lobes (where concepts such as time are sensed). At least that's the committed view of a section of the medical establishment, although there are plenty of professionals willing to dismiss ADD as a fad, perhaps to excuse low achievement or as a chance to sell medication.

Nonetheless, there are clearly personal characteristics that can be grouped as a 'condition' that detrimentally impacts our ability to organize ourselves productively, whether we diagnose it as ADD or not.

According to Dr Marilyn Paul in *Why Am I So Disorganized?* (2009) these can include:

- an inability to focus on anything for longer than a moment,
- problems attending to one task at a time,
- being easily distracted,
- impulsiveness,
- beginning many projects simultaneously, but finishing few,
- scrambling to meet deadlines, despite long lead times,
- a tendency to procrastinate,
- a tendency to be moody or experience mood swings,
- thriving in high-stimulation situations,
- enjoying novelty, and
- a tendency to need immediate reinforcement or confirmation.

## Distractibility, impulsiveness and risk-taking

Other writers – including psychotherapist Thom Hartmann in *Healing ADD* (1998) – focus on just three primary ADD behaviours: distractibility, impulsiveness and risk-taking.

'These three characteristics show up in a variety of ways', writes Hartmann, 'ranging from general disorganization to procrastination to difficulties in school and relationships.'

Yet there's no agreed diagnosis. There's not even an agreed name, with the more popular iteration now being ADHD (with ADD viewed as a 'predominantly inattentive' subtype reclassified as ADHD-PI). When considering the unproductive mind, however, hyperactivity is an unnecessary (and potentially misleading) trait, making ADD a more helpful label for our purposes.

Of course, ADD is not an all-or-nothing disorder. It occupies a spectrum of severity, although all the tests developed in the 1990s (when ADD became a diagnosable condition) agree that the symptoms must have been lifelong, rather than the result of some adult event (such as an illness or accident), and must be severe enough to represent, as Hartmann states, a 'significant step away from the norm'.

## The hunter of pre-history

ADD is sometimes described as a by-product of an inattentive modern world seeking instant gratification. Meanwhile, others assume it's a genetic disorder – pointing to a high incidence of inherited behaviours. In fact, according to Oliver James in his book on family survival called *They F*** You Up* (2002), around three million American children are on medication (usually Ritalin) for ADD/ADHD, based on the assumption that it's a disease with a potentially genetic root cause (something James disputes).

Yet Hartmann offers an alternative view. Sufferers are normal human beings with normal behavioural instincts, he claims. They've simply been unable to adjust their instinctive behaviour to suit our unnatural, urban, post-industrial lives. In his theory, ADD is no more than a psychological leftover from a world that's moved too far from the hunter-gatherer 'state of nature'.

'I'd noticed early on that the cardinal characteristics of ADD – distractibility, impulsivity, and a love of novelty/sensation/risk – were all things which would be adaptive in a society where food was acquired by hunting and gathering', writes Hartmann. 'The "distractible" hunter would constantly be scanning the forest or jungle as he looked for food and watched out for dangers and predators.'

So, while such behaviour looks maladjusted in the classroom – and becomes viewed as a problem – on the savannah of pre-history, the same impulses would have been vital for survival, a theory Hartmann supports by citing recent studies of the few remaining hunter-gatherer societies.

As a theory, this certainly feels right to me (and we'll deal below with the fact this appears to exclude half the population) – especially as it helps us reframe the negative and self-esteem-sapping consequences of such a label.

## Normal human behaviour

That said, as an adult, an ADD/ADHD diagnosis can feel comforting – as an explanatory moment when contradictory behaviours at last make sense.

'ADD seemed to explain many of my behaviour patterns, thought processes, childish emotional reactions, my workaholism and other addictive tendencies, the sudden eruptions of bad temper and complete irrationality, the conflicts in my marriage, and my Jekyll and Hyde ways of relating to my children', writes Canadian physician Gabor Maté MD, author of *Scattered* (2000). 'Beyond everything it revealed the reason for my life-long sense of somehow never approaching my potential in terms of self-expression and self-definition – the ADD adult's awareness that he has talents . . . he could perhaps connect with if the wires weren't crossed.'

Certainly, Maté's description resonates. Yet it also reveals a misunderstanding about ADD characteristics, or unproductive or disorganized behaviour generally: motivation. Indeed, of Hartmann's many case studies one stood out for me – of a youth in the north of England who'd become a social problem – getting into fights or trouble with the police, being thrown out of school, drunkenly raging against the world and generally terrorizing his family and the neighbourhood.

'Richard has ADD', said his mother, 'he is completely unmotivated. He doesn't want to do a damn thing.'

Yet when quizzed by Hartmann, the boy revealed strong motivation for a range of activities including drinking beer, loitering with his friends, driving fast (perhaps stolen) cars and skateboarding. Motivation was not the issue, Hartmann concluded. It was the direction of his motivation that was problematic (at least for others).

This certainly concurs with my own experiences. From an early age I indulged in antisocial activities – including shoplifting and petty vandalism – that had me marked down as a 'problem'. Yet, despite the view of my teachers, I was far from unmotivated. Even as a young child I could invest time and energy creating and completing tasks requiring highly detailed levels of organization. Put me in the garden and I'd invent and build a complex maze for my pet guinea-pig to navigate. With friends, I'd dream up convoluted plans for stealthily traversing the back gardens of the neighbourhood. Even when left alone in my bedroom, my collection of marbles became a new and highly specialized sport involving elaborate rules and international teams.

And the levels of complexity grew the older I became. From the age of ten, I mentally occupied my own made-up country: a scaled-up version of my neighbourhood (in which my village became a city and the local town a metropolis). Enlivened by the excitement of this private world, I was soon doctoring local maps to create coastlines and physical features and – before long – was writing and drawing my country's unique geography, history and economy. The detail was extraordinary: transport maps, government department budgets, national symbolism and heritage – even election results, newspaper headlines and football squads. Every aspect of this country was recorded in a logical and accessible order after hours spent in creative thought and detailed analysis.

So, it's not motivation that's lacking from the unproductive person, or the ability to order their lives (when motivated to do so). Often it's simply a resistance to formalized – imposed – structure. To those with ADD characteristics, such impositions feel abnormal: like a mental imprisonment. In fact, many can be thrown (rather than helped) by organizational aids such as a to-do list or daily plan or appointment book. They become just another barrier – something else banging on their unconscious door as a reminder of their 'deficit'.

As we plot our path towards productivity, therefore, we need to remain acutely aware of this. Formal structures imposed upon us may simply build our resistance to organization. We have to ensure they're *our* structures – suited to *our* needs – and aimed at securing *our* goals.

## Women and ADD

But have we forgotten half the population? The traits above – and certainly their potential roots in early society – have an undoubtedly masculine bent. Indeed, much of the original focus on ADD – and current focus with ADHD – suggests this may be an exclusively male concern. Yet researchers and physicians now accept this is far from a boys-only malaise.

'ADD can have a profound impact on women, perhaps even greater than its effect on men', wrote David B. Sudderth MD and Joseph Kandel MD in their 1996 book *Adult ADD – the Complete Handbook*.

One reason offered for the oversight is the fact girls are far less likely to exhibit hyperactivity, which is frequently seen in boys and is, perhaps, the most outwardly noticeable trait (although, as stated, a far from universal one). Another is that girls with ADD characteristics often have more acute self-esteem concerns, according to Sudderth and Kandel, and this may form the focus of parental or professional concern.

Even accepting Hartmann's pre-history hunter theory (as I do) shouldn't exclude girls. Surviving hunter-gatherer groups in both Asia and Africa – such as the Aeta in the Philippines – reveal that the majority of women also hunt. And anthropologist Stephen L. Kuhn of the University of Arizona has suggested that gender-specific roles (such as the hunting and gathering division) only emerged in the Upper Paleolithic era (i.e. late Stone Age), which can be as recent as 10,000 years ago.

So ADD characteristics can undoubtedly exist (or develop) in girls and can have a major impact on female adults – especially when trying to juggle the multiple responsibilities that so often become the woman's role in the family home. Poor productivity at this level can also lead to enhanced feelings of guilt and inadequacy because women feel they're letting down others, while the male version is usually more focused on the personal consequences.

And, for women and men, we must also be aware that the modern world – while not necessarily to blame – is unlikely to improve our distractibility, with contemporary office jobs exacerbating rather than soothing our organizational deficiencies.

## Asperger's syndrome – more than just low empathy

Yet we're far from done with the conditions potentially impacting our productivity. First up: Asperger's syndrome, named after the Austrian paediatrician who studied childhood traits such as poor nonverbal communication skills, limited empathy with others and physical clumsiness – later banded together as a diagnosable condition.

Debate rages regarding what characteristics are included as part of an Asperger's diagnosis, although most sources accept the following:

- a lack of demonstrable empathy, especially in immediate situations,
- difficulty developing meaningful or mutual friendships,
- poor reciprocity in conversation – including indulging in monologues (or 'talking at' people),
- difficulties with social interaction and poor social intuition,
- uninhibited verbalization of thoughts, including potentially hurtful or tactless statements,
- awkward social skills, such as intense eye contact or inappropriate facial expressions,
- poor or misleading voice intonation – including oddities in volume and pitch,
- intense preoccupancy with narrow subjects – potentially to the extent of being considered mildly autistic (in fact, Asperger's is on the World Health Organization's 'autism spectrum' of pervasive developmental disorders),

- physical clumsiness and inelegant limb coordination,
- impaired humour appreciation – including a low awareness of non-literal language such as irony or sarcasm,
- differences in perception with others witnessing the same event – although often with an enhanced perception of (not always significant) details,
- dislike of even minimal change, with a potentially extreme preference for routines and rituals,
- unusual sensitivity to light or sound or other stimuli, making them appear restless and distracted,
- sensory processing inconsistencies – meaning they can both over-respond (perhaps being majorly concerned by background noise) and under-respond (perhaps not noticing when they are being directly addressed),
- sleep disorders, and early morning awakenings,
- deficits in task fulfilment involving visual-spatial perception, or auditory perception.

And while only the last of these traits is directly linked to poor productivity, difficulties with sensory processing can prevent a sufferer from managing sustained and focused attention. Also, an obsession with particular – and potentially irrelevant – details can act as a barrier to planning and progress, as can a preference for ritualistic routine. In fact, children and adolescents with Asperger's are prone to poor levels of self-care and organization. Many delay leaving home, procrastinate with respect to major decisions or projects and are disturbed by change.

As to the causes, Hans Asperger himself noticed that family members – especially fathers – tended to share the same characteristics, which has, again, led to suggestions of a genetic condition, although no gene has ever been discovered. Certainly, other autism spectrum disorders are mostly viewed as genetic by the medical establishment, although there are plenty of observers (including Oliver James) who think that environmental factors (such as family life) play a more significant role.

## Other disorders

Of course, many people reading the above will have mentally ticked off the characteristics to conclude that they have Asperger's syndrome. I certainly did. But then I did for ADD. And then I read about 'simple schizophrenia' (sometimes known as 'disorganization syndrome' or 'deteriorative disorder') and thought I had that as well. Characteristics – according to London-based psychologists Susannah Whitwell, Jessica Bramham and John Moriarty, writing in *Advances in Psychiatric Treatment* (a journal of the Royal College of Psychiatrists) – include:

- poor interaction and sociability resulting in withdrawal,
- difficulties in planning or making decisions,
- chaotic behaviour (including lateness and an ability to obey rules),
- low threshold for verbal aggression,
- difficulties in initiating actions, or in completing tasks once initiated, and
- behavioural disinhibition – perhaps resulting in a poor awareness of appropriate behavioural boundaries.

The reference to 'simple' is due to the lack of hallucinations or delusions usually associated with schizophrenia, and it differs from Asperger's or other autism-spectrum disorders due to the fact the condition develops in people previously seen as 'normal'.

Yet there are plenty more disorders where these came from. Another condition, which gained traction in the 1990s, is myalgic encephalomyelitis (ME) now more commonly known as chronic fatigue syndrome (CFS). Again, not without its controversies, symptoms mostly occur after periods of extreme stress or in the recovery period from a flu-like illness, which has led to speculation that CFS is linked to a virus or series of viruses (although recent studies have 'disproved' the link). Fatigue and muscle pain persist – for as long as six months or a year – and are accompanied by psychological characteristics such as depression, mood swings, irritability, anxiety and panic attacks. The result: impaired information processing and a decrease in attention span, memory, reaction time and motivation.

Next up: obsessive compulsive disorder (OCD) – an anxiety disorder in which potentially harmful or inappropriate obsessions are countered by compulsive behaviours (for instance an obsession with germs can lead to compulsive hand-washing). And this can result in diverting behaviours that pose a significant barrier to our productive and organizational pursuits.

Then there's dysmorphophobia (an anxiety disorder leading to withdrawal, poor social functioning and low motivation often due to an obsession with a small – perhaps facial – disfigurement); bipolar disorder (where energetic, even euphoric, episodes of lucid creativity are followed by depression, self-loathing and inaction); childhood disintegrative disorder or Heller's syndrome (in which development in self-care functionality or social skills regresses as the child ages), seasonal affective disorder (in which seasonal change generates a depressed and demotivated state), and executive dysfunction (a neurobiological condition affecting planning, sequencing, organizing, initiating and self-monitoring skills), and so on . . .

Eventually, the world of disorders capable of negatively impacting our organizational competence starts resembling a Savile Row tailor, in which we can all be measured for a near-bespoke mental ailment to explain away our deficiencies.

## MBTI types

And we may not have any form of disorder. We may simply be a type. Certainly, Katherine Cook Briggs and her daughter Isabel Briggs Myers would have us think so. They created the Myers-Briggs Type Indicator (MBTI) in the 1940s, initially to help women entering the workplace during the war years to choose appropriate employment preferences. Today, MBTI is the world's most widely used psychometric (i.e. the measurement of psychological traits) questionnaire – adopted by human resources departments across the globe as a 'reliable' universal test of employee suitability.

The types originate from the psychological theories of Carl Jung who considered humans divisible with respect to how they process information and evaluate the world. Jung considered these divisions hardwired – based on the accumulation of many generations of behaviour, especially in particular societies. MBTI proponents also insist there's no right and wrong or better or worse 'type', although it quickly becomes apparent certain types have a propensity for stronger productivity than others.

While too complex to explain in full, in essence MBTIs divide people into groups selected by a combination of answers to either/or questions. Various permutations of these choices – combined with a calculation regarding which preferences dominate – determine our personality type.

For instance, when 'making decisions' (one of four key MBTI determinants) we're invited to choose between our preference for 'thinking' or 'feeling'. Thinkers like to decide things from a detached, logical and reason-based standpoint. Meanwhile, feelers tend to come to decisions using their emotions. They look for empathy and harmony and 'fit'.

With respect to our 'favourite world' (another key determinant) we have to choose between being 'extraverts' and 'introverts'. Those preferring 'extraversion' like to act, then reflect, then act further based on the results. Their motivation declines if they're inactive. Introverts, however, prefer to reflect, then act, and then reflect again. Extraverts direct their energy to people and objects, while introverts direct it towards ideas.

And then there's 'sensing' or 'intuition' – our decision with respect to 'dealing with information'. Those who prefer sensing are more likely to trust concrete information. They distrust hunches while liking facts and figures. Intuition-oriented individuals, meanwhile, prefer theoretical or abstract information.

The MBTI tests result in the award of one of 16 types, described in terms of four-letter acronyms. Yet the types are always described positively, which means we must read between the lines to discern the negatives. For instance, ENFPs are extraverted, intuitive, feeling and perceptive, which means they're sociable, imaginative, outspoken and personable. Yet that may also mean they're bored by routine and seldom able to repeat the same task in the same way, which – while making them apt to adopt many new interests – also makes them strong candidates for being inattentive thrill-seekers.

ISTJs, by contrast, are introverted, sensing, thinking and judgemental. They are quiet and serious, thorough and dependable. They are practical, orderly, logical, decisive and able to work steadily towards a planned goal, which makes them unlikely candidates for a book aimed at unproductive and organizationally dysfunctional people.

## Are types useful?

There are two million assessments undertaken annually according to the company that publishes the MBTI test, so they clearly work at some level – perhaps helping major employers differentiate between academically-similar candidates. But the tests have their detractors, who most often focus on the lack of critical scrutiny of the outcomes. Some statisticians point out that the score distributions reveal abnormalities, while others point to the terminology being vague, the descriptions being too brief to be meaningful and the tests being open to dishonest reporting.

And then there's the fact that a large percentage (estimates range from 36–76 percent) of those tested fall into a different category when retested, perhaps just weeks later – all of which leads critics such as psychologist David Pittenger to wonder about the usefulness of those 'beguiling . . . horoscope-like summaries'.

Indeed, just like zodiacal signs, it's easy to accept your type and then search your personal history for traits that confirm your classification – a bit like all those conditions, in fact.

**Get Things Done:** *Diagnosed or not, disorders such as ADD and Asperger's can have a major impact on our potential for productivity – whatever the root causes of the conditions. Or we may be an MBTI type, although both types and conditions have self-fulfilling qualities that we need to guard against.*

# 3

# PROCRASTINATION, CLUTTER AND SELF-SABOTAGE

There's a propensity to over-diagnose the conditions described in the previous chapter – something nearly all the experts admit. Indeed, many unproductive people are keen to be diagnosed, perhaps preferring a comforting label to explain their discomforting deficiencies. Yet, in my opinion, there's one condition at the heart of many (but not all) of those diagnosed with conditions such as ADD: low self-esteem.

It's low self-esteem that destroys our motivation, with even small setbacks viewed as confirmation of our negative self-beliefs – little wonder we'd rather hide behind some diagnosable condition.

According to John Caunt, author of *Boost Your Self-Esteem* (2002), it's the self-beliefs we develop in childhood that generate high or low self-esteem. These are reinforced by those around us: from their feedback as well as their love and acceptance, or indeed their enmity or intolerance. If negative, our inner self-beliefs prevent us from developing the high self-esteem that's a key ingredient for generating strong achievement-focused habits, including deferred gratification.

Our default setting is that we're worthless: a reference point that can reassert itself no matter how far down the line we've travelled.

Indeed – given such destructive self-beliefs – we can end up scouring the horizon for confirmation of our poor self-assessment, no matter what our external attainments.

According to Caunt, low self-esteem can present itself in many ways, including:

- doing things solely to win the approval of others,
- constantly comparing ourselves to others and resenting those that succeed,
- feeling like a failure and always focusing on the negative,
- being overly-sensitive to criticism – indeed, allowing even constructive criticism to derail us,
- giving in to others' desires,
- avoiding actions for fear of failure and public humiliation,
- striving for unrealistic levels of perfection,
- worrying excessively – but not asking for help,
- putting ourselves down, even in public,
- feeling out of control,
- withdrawing from people or social events,
- becoming aggressive or overly passive,
- punishing ourselves – or only allowing ourselves to 'earn' feelings of well-being.

## The toxic internal critic

And while much of the above may not look that devastating for our productivity, it is.

'When you reject parts of yourself, you greatly damage the psychological structures that literally keep you alive', write San Francisco-based psychologists Matthew McKay and Patrick Fanning in *Self-Esteem* (2000). 'The pathological critic [inside you] is busy undermining your self-worth every day of your life. Yet his voice is so insidious, so woven into the fabric of your thought that you never notice its devastating effect.'

According to McKay and Fanning, this toxic internal critic destroys objectivity, undermines positivity and kills motivation stone dead. It's also self-fulfilling: creating the circumstances that confirm its own predictions of failure and defeat. Sure, we may try to excuse our behaviour – even diagnose it differently in order to avoid the painful realization that it's our own self-beliefs that are causing the problems. We can even try to mask it via self-destructive behaviour such as anger, withdrawal, bravado or rebelliousness – or numb the pain through licentiousness, addictions or gluttony. But, ultimately, there's no escape: we're the ones driving our own behaviour thanks to our own – disastrous – self-beliefs.

Even today, as someone with low self-esteem, I find writing on this subject painful. Here I am, in my late 40s, having to accept that I'm responsible for my own dysfunctionality – brought about due to poor self-beliefs that reach right back to my early childhood. And, no matter how much I try to shift the blame, as an adult I must accept full responsibility for the impact this has had on my progress.

I've sabotaged myself: from poor planning, poor goal-setting and poor execution – based on my inner beliefs that I was neither capable, nor deserving, of such progress.

Maslow had it right. I've been so busy seeking the love and approval I lacked in my childhood, I've been incapable of motivating myself towards the self-actualization of productive pursuits. Instead, I lost myself in a fantasy country where I could be the prime minister, the national football coach and the editor of the leading newspaper rolled into one. And while I could have acquired any number of labels to explain my incompetence, I didn't even have the wherewithal to get myself diagnosed – something I now consider in my favour. Lacking the convenience of a 'condition', I've finally – in middle life – developed a blinding clarity regarding how I got myself into this position.

Just maybe those disorders are unhelpful to our cause: as is any indication of personality type. Such avenues can result in self-fulfilling adult dysfunctionality, with us hiding behind statements such as 'that's just the way I am' or 'I can't help myself' that strip away our autonomy with respect to our own productivity.

Only once we've grasped our own role in our dysfunctionality can we develop productive and organizational competence. And this means that our best bet may be to do the opposite to what we've previously done. Instead, of attaching ourselves to some condition by searching our memories for incidents that comply with their symptoms, we should focus on the points where we differ. What characteristics do we *not* share? It's these points we should look for and linger upon.

For instance, I enjoy rather than fear novelty, which would make ADD rather than Asperger's my condition – reinforced by the fact I've no problem with empathy. Cartoons and even dog-food adverts can have me fighting back the tears, meaning that – if I can gain empathy with fictional animals and even computer-generated pixels – Asperger's is certainly not my concern.

And then there's the fact I can show almost autistic levels of concentration on seemingly irrelevant subjects (such as made-up countries), which is beyond the usual experience of those with ADD, making me an unlikely candidate there too. As for simple schizophrenia – well I certainly don't think I was ever 'normal'. I've always felt incapable of strong, productive, organizational competence. OCD, CFS, SAD? Perhaps, but most likely not.

Just maybe I'm Robert Kelsey: a complex human-being looking for a label to explain away my poor productivity and organizational dysfunctionality when, in reality, it's no more than my negative self-beliefs, caused by low self-esteem.

## Self-belief: the missing ingredient

For me, and I suspect for many who examine themselves honestly, there's always been something missing. And that something, I'm now convinced, is self-belief. We inwardly think we're incapable of strong, self-motivated achievement, so we prove ourselves right – looking (and therefore finding) the evidence that supports this predisposition. Painful as this is to confess, we have to accept that we're our own worst enemy when it comes to organizing ourselves for effective progress.

Yet this isn't the disaster it seems. If we're responsible for getting ourselves into this mess, we're responsible for getting ourselves out of it. It's in *our* hands. Also, if low self-esteem is the crucial differentiator, then we have a major benchmark for our success as a goal-oriented and productive person. Low self-esteem has resulted in organizational dysfunctionality, so becoming organizationally competent – and therefore more productive – should surely undermine our poor self-beliefs, which is immediately a worthwhile and motivating pursuit. This is about shaking off the most crippling characteristic of our personality: our negative, disabling and self-fulfilling self-beliefs.

And this should have a major impact when dealing with two of the primary symptoms of our malaise: procrastination and clutter.

## The Procrastinator's Code

The dictionary definition of procrastination is simply 'to defer', 'to delay' or 'to put off until tomorrow' – a tendency of one in four adults, according to University of California psychologists Jane B. Burka and Lonora M. Yuen in their classic text *Procrastination* (1983).

Burka and Yuen are at pains to point out that procrastination doesn't usually stem from laziness, irresponsibility or lack of discipline. In fact, the roots are rather familiar.

'The emotional roots of procrastination involve inner feelings, fears, hopes, memories, dreams, doubts and pressures', they write.

Life's challenges scare procrastinators, claim Burka and Yuen – a fear that most often comes from their inner feelings of low self-esteem. Such feelings produce results such as fear and catastrophic thinking, which may be rooted in a poor or stressful upbringing, or even traumas in young adulthood, they claim, although they don't dismiss the idea of genetic inheritance. Whatever the cause, the outcome is a series of mistaken all-or-nothing ideas, including:

- I must be perfect,
- everything I do should go easily,
- it's safer to do nothing, than risk failure,
- I should have no limitations,
- if it's not done right, it's not worth doing,
- I must avoid being challenged,
- if I succeed, someone will get hurt,
- if I do well this time, I must always do well,
- following others' rules means I'm giving in,
- I can't afford to let go of anyone or anything,
- if I show my real self, I'll be disliked,
- there's a right answer, which I'm waiting to find.

This is what Burka and Yuen call the *Procrastinator's Code*: fear-generated thinking that produces a desire to consciously or unconsciously delay life's challenges.

'Many people who procrastinate are apprehensive about being judged by others or by the critic who dwells within,' they write.

Of course, there's also an internal cost. Procrastinators can suffer from feelings that range from irritation and regret to intense self-condemnation and despair. Yet many also generate self-confirming excuses to hide the consequences of their behaviour – such as the idea that, although capable, they simply don't have the time to execute future-oriented projects.

For most, however, procrastination hides deep convictions of unworthiness that can manifest themselves as not wanting to 'showcase ambition' or a fear of the commitments required from achievement, or simply feelings that 'I don't deserve success'. And some procrastinators are – despite appearances – seeking control, which means digging in their heels against what they see as outside pressures – perhaps through unconscious (although deliberate) tardiness or stubbornness.

Burka and Yuen focus on conditioning as both a cause and potential relief for procrastination, stating that – while negative or painful childhood experiences may have generated the inability to focus on and execute future-oriented actions – the brain is an 'ever-changing biological entity'. It constantly builds new neural connections and disengages old ones, making it capable of developing new patterns and habits that can remove our propensity for tardiness or inaction (more on habits in Part Two). While procrastination may be our default response – hardwired into us for whatever reason – new habits *can* emerge from new conditioning.

'You have a choice,' conclude Burka and Yuen. 'You can delay or you can act.'

## Clutter – the not so benign symptom

As for clutter, what can sound like a minor irritation, can – according to clutter-guru Mike Nelson, author of *Stop Clutter From Stealing Your Life* (2001) – be a symptom of a major psychological disorder. A disorder, what's more, that can destroy self-esteem, relationships and careers, as well as lead to financial problems.

Of course, the word clutter generates images of dusty attics and cobwebbed sheds – or maybe a kindly uncle's book-laden study. Yet it can be far more disabling. Clutter can clog whole aspects of our lives and lead to potentially disastrous consequences: our financial affairs – including our taxes – could be in disarray due to our inability to cut through the mountain of paper, as can utility payments, work projects and career advancements. Even the pleasurable aspects of our lives – such as friendships and holidays – can find themselves utterly cluttered (see Part Three). For instance, we could make too many conflicting arrangements, or we could maintain destructive or unenjoyable pursuits for fear of change.

'For most people a desk littered with papers or a closet or garage stuffed with forgotten items is a mild annoyance', writes Nelson. 'For clutterers, it is an outward manifestation of our inner lives.

Inside, we're afraid of losing love [a notion Maslow would find familiar], so we hang onto every object that comes into our lives.'

Far from seeking release, says Nelson, most clutterers find self-esteem-supporting excuses for indulging their clutter. These can include:

- I am an artist and artists are messy.
- I am a genius. We are allowed.
- I am [insert nationality]. It's part of our culture.

Unfortunately, Nelson states, the true reasons for cluttering are more to do with deep feelings of insecurity. Because we feel we deserve no better, we cling to the things we have – including relationships. Or we inwardly convince ourselves that these things are irreplaceable.

Other clutterer convictions, according to Nelson (with some thoughts of my own), include:

- *Feeling unloved.* We fill our lives with things (even activities or people) to replace the love we lack or fear we'll lose.
- *Feeling 'less than'.* We fill our lives to make us feel prettier, cooler, smarter, more successful than we inwardly feel. 'Here's my stuff', we seem to be saying, 'judge that, not me'.
- *Listening to old tapes.* As children, many of us were told we weren't good enough – would never amount to much. Yet this is a self-fulfilling prophecy fed to us by psychologically ignorant people. Here, clutter can act as our umbilical cord to the past – perhaps always looking for a better result or the approval that will never come.
- *Saving for a rainy day.* Our parents may have known rationing or the straightened times of economic hardship. Indeed, previous generations may have been conditioned to hoard (revealed in behaviours such as saving Christmas wrapping paper), and have passed on these values. Within limits, such values are positive. Mixed with other insecurities, however, they can become barriers to our progress.

- *Feeling overwhelmed.* All those bills piling up, all those unanswered emails, all those commitments being pressed upon us – it feels like a *tsunami* of other people's requirements. Such pressures generate an emotional, even fearful, reaction that reinforces our feelings of inadequacy. Rather than take control, we do the opposite. We mentally (and sometimes physically) run away.
- *Feeling guilty.* Both ways – guilty for having the junk or having the unresolved or conflicting commitments, and guilty for throwing it away or saying 'no'.
- *Feeling like a failure.* This is actually a sign of recovery, according to Nelson, because it's the next step on from the 'less than' feeling – the realization that our clutter is harming us and that we must, therefore, do something about it.
- *Feeling confused.* Nelson cites Lynda Warren, a Californian psychologist, describing clutterers as people that have difficulties making decisions. They are incapable of focus, and their cluttered lives reveal their inner confusion. No one has given them a map, so they lack direction and, therefore, cannot judge what they need, and don't need, for their journey; hence they hoard.

## Snatching defeat from the jaws of victory

All of which makes cluttering a more disabling trait than it first appears. Indeed, combined with procrastination, cluttering forms part of what clinical psychotherapist Pat Pearson terms 'self-sabotage' in which we actually adopt behaviours with the specific intention (perhaps unconsciously) of destroying our own progress.

This could be in our dealings with others – perhaps telling them our weaknesses before they find out through observation (in the hope they'll treat us kindly). Or it could be in our actions – perhaps by playing the fool or deliberately missing appointments (maybe due to fear of failure).

Why would we do this? According to Pearson, in his book *Stop Self-Sabotage* (2008), we're – yet again – dealing with low self-esteem and the belief systems that we developed in childhood. If we believe we're not worthy of success (however measured), we'll adopt behaviours that prevent it.

These can include (with some thoughts of my own):

- *Throwing it away.* Falling victim to post-achievement destructive behaviour due to being 'uncomfortable' with success is a classic symptom of low self-esteem. Pearson cites the high divorce rates among pro-football stars in the US, although self-destructive, celebrity-style behaviour is common even in non-celebrity circles if success feels inwardly undeserved or perhaps ephemeral.
- *Settling for less.* We may stop short of our stated goals because our inner convictions assume we're unworthy of further attainment. Or we could 'snatch defeat from the jaws of victory' by sabotaging that final step – a common outcome for those with low self-esteem who may inwardly feel themselves unworthy of the benefits of attainment (and a very common problem for me).
- *Resignation.* We can even give in to the negative self-talk, which means we're defeated before we've even begun. A classic example is avoiding talking to an attractive stranger because we assume they'll find us unworthy of their engagement. Avoiding contested promotions in the workplace is part of the same dynamic, as is a compulsion to bring up our weaknesses at important job interviews. It's as if we're saying: 'I know what you think, I agree, but please take pity'.
- *The fatal flaw.* Perfectionism, procrastination, narcissism (constantly requiring others' admiration): all are examples of a psychological flaw that, if ignored, could lead to self-sabotage despite strong progress. Pearson cites former US president Bill Clinton, whose one-parent upbringing potentially led to his narcissistic and self-destructive behaviour with Monica Lewinsky.

- *Denial.* The avoidance of unwanted or unpleasant truths can mean we minimize issues, or rationalize poor choices or behaviours, or even blame others: all forms of denial. And such behaviour can lead to a painful reckoning as the consequences of our actions crash over us (perhaps when others finally snap).

## Deserve levels

'As long as your unconscious mind is allowed to do the assessing and strategizing in your life, it becomes the spoiler', writes Pearson, 'able to generate a continual supply of self-sabotaging "strategies" that turn roads into ruts in your life.'

According to Pearson, such behaviours are based on where we set our 'deserve levels', which are fixed in childhood and may have been suppressed by demeaning parents, siblings, teachers or peers. The moment we cross that mental threshold, we move beyond our 'comfort zone' and subconsciously employ self-sabotaging tactics to bring us back down.

'Your history is written deeply into your psyche', says Pearson.

And unless you make strong efforts to raise your 'deserve levels' and tackle your own self-sabotaging behaviours, he believes, it will also determine your future.

That said, such a result is far from inevitable.

**Get Things Done:** *The key reason for our poor productivity or organizational incompetence is low self-esteem. Indeed, self-esteem lies at the heart of the two key symptoms of our unproductive state: procrastination and clutter. Both may involve elements of self-sabotage, because of our inner convictions regarding what we deserve.*

# 4

# MOTIVATION, GOALS AND FLOW

It's at this point that many self-help writers make statements such as 'get a grip' or 'take control'. Certainly, taking responsibility for our predicament is a major step, and one many – even those reading self-help books – fail to make. We can be too busy blaming others for our failures and shortcomings to realize that the only person responsible for our future is us. It's in our hands, as long as we make the decision to grasp it.

Such a decision is a key moment in our journey towards salvation from our unproductive state. It's an epiphany we must experience.

Self-help guru, Brian Tracy, wrote of his own epiphany in *Goals!* (2003).

'One night as I sat at my small kitchen table, I had a great flash of awareness', he wrote. 'It changed my life. I suddenly realized that everything that would happen to me for the rest of my life was going to be up to me. No one else was going to help me. *No one was coming to the rescue.*'

Anyone seeking productive organizational competence needs to experience something similar. Disorganization, procrastination, clutter, cynicism – even anger, depression and distrust: all are symptoms of a malaise of our own making in which our poor self-beliefs (however acquired) have been translated into disabling inaction or self-sabotaging action.

No matter what our personal histories, we must realize that we got ourselves into this position and only we can get ourselves out of it. Yet by accepting this – perhaps via some enlightened Tracy-style moment of clarity or, as happened to me, with the friend I trusted finally snapping and shouting some home truths – we're making the first move towards a more productive future. This is the moment we become adults: realizing that, unless we deal with our own disabling attitudes and habits (fostered by our poor self-beliefs), they're going to hinder us for the rest of our lives.

## Motivation is the key

Of course, motivation is the key. Motivation regulates all animal behaviour and, unless we have it – and more importantly sustain it – we're going nowhere. So far, we may have been motivated by fear, fuelled by the disabling self-beliefs that tell us our ambitions are mere dreams and that our fate is our current disorganized and demotivated state. Yet that was the past. As for the future – well, nothing's ordained unless we assume it so. Our past dictates our future only if we allow it. Refuse to accept such a verdict and the future is an open book; one we can fill as we please as long as we're motivated to do so.

'If you are doing something, pursuing something or achieving something, you are somehow motivated to do it, pursue it or achieve it', writes author Tom Gorman in his groundbreaking book *Motivation* (2007). 'Motivation ignites, energizes, determines, directs and explains our behaviour.'

Gorman cites the enemies of motivation as 'feeling undeserving' (we are not worthy of progress), 'fear' (of failure and humiliation), 'comparisons' (with peers or parents) and 'blame' ('it was our upbringing' etc.). As we've seen, these are our self-beliefs, which may be hardwired into us from past experiences. And developing new beliefs is the most difficult element of any programme towards personal change because there are no words or exercises that can remove these feelings and insecurities – no matter what the claims of hypnotists or acupuncturists or other purveyors of quick-fix solutions.

In fact, our desire for quick-fix solutions – even those found in self-help books – can be a further form of denial: an admission that we think ourselves incapable of change and must, therefore, recruit someone else's power to assist us. Yet, in my view, this is no more than a delayed reckoning. Sure, it may initially work because we've adopted the characteristics of someone with positive self-beliefs. Give it time, however – and perhaps a few setbacks – and our quick-fix solutions will turn out to be no fix at all, just further confirmation of our negative self-beliefs.

Our negative self-beliefs are therefore part of us, which means they're coming with us on our journey. This is an important realization because it may well be these insecurities that have prevented us from taking action thus far. We wait for them to go away – potentially spending a fortune on cures or treatments in our desire to exorcize the demon. Yet they won't go away because they can't.

So, we have a choice: fruitlessly wait for our fears and insecurities to disappear, or accept them as fellow passengers and take them into account as we move forward.

## Plan-beliefs replace self-beliefs

What has this got to do with motivation? Well, our negative self-beliefs have acted to kill positive motivation, so we need something to replace self-belief as a motivational tool. Of course, poor self-beliefs must be navigated, or even accommodated – something we can achieve by replacing self-belief with faith in our plans. If we generate a plan for our future, and then invest belief in that plan, it might just allow us to ignore our disabling *self*-beliefs.

From here on, it's no longer about us. It's about them: our plans, which are unemotional projects involving objectives and tasks.

For this to work, however, plans must – indeed – be motivational, which means they must reflect our values. They also need to be detailed and credible. But, as we shall see, such elements are easily added. It's execution that throws up the difficulties, although even here our progress is eased with the aid of some strong plans.

Certainly, believing in our plans makes a world of difference. Plans get us off the starting blocks and give us direction. They also give our actions meaning, which can help overcome fear.

But effective plans must start with an objective. And that requires goals.

'Goals move you from the realm of dreams into reality', says Gorman (2007). 'Goals focus your motivation on things you can achieve and obtain in the real world, [not] things you think that you would do if only the world, or you, were different.'

No matter how many books I've read on motivation, or on becoming more productive or achieving success or simply improving my life, not one has contradicted this message. Goals matter. Goals get us up in the morning and act as motivational fuel to see us through the setbacks and frustrations. Goals also give us judgement (something many of us previously lacked) by acting as a benchmark for our decisions. And goals give us belief because, if we know where we're going – and are motivated to go there – how can we fail to take the necessary steps towards our destination? Steps, what's more, that – over time and with strong self-reinforcement – help us make progress despite our poor self-beliefs.

## Seven key steps for goal-setting

In his landmark book, *Motivation and Goal-Setting* (1998), life-coach Jim Cairo sets out his thoughts on goal-setting. I've added my own thoughts, as well as those of Brian Tracy, Anthony Robbins, Tom Gorman, Stephen Covey and many other self-help gurus, to offer what I see as the seven key steps for goal-setting.

1. *Goals should excite you.* Many people set goals that are designed to please others (peers or parents perhaps) or are based on influences fed to them, maybe from popular culture. Yet these goals will fail to motivate you over the long term because they're not *your* goals. So what really gets you going? What excites your interest or even your anger (perhaps your sense of injustice)? What parts of a newspaper do you read first? What magazines or websites grab your attention? You should consider such things when you look at what drives you, and set long-term goals on this basis. Just maybe you're stuck because you don't truly value your pursuits. For instance, my goal to qualify as a building surveyor was in reality my father's goal. To do so, I had to take evening A-level classes and chose history, which so fired me up I achieved an 'A' grade and eventually a university degree in the subject (after abandoning a building surveying course that failed to motivate me).
2. *Goals should reflect your values.* Yet you need to look deeper than pure excitement, which may dissipate as the going gets tough. Removing the motivating thrill of excitement from your long-term goal-setting isn't easy. But it's possible with the aid of your values. What deep-rooted and unshakable views do you hold? Are you highly competitive and determined to win, or are you more worried about the loser's feelings? Is your own work important, or are you keener to encourage others? Do you value aesthetics more than mechanics? Function over form? Life more than art? These are the foundations for your long-term goal-setting. It's from this basis that goals become sustainable, even inevitable. For instance, if you're sincere about improving health, then goals involving medicine will feel sustainable, meaning you should resist family pressure to become an accountant. Artists should follow art, sportspeople sports, mathematicians maths. That said, this is deeper than desire: it's your core being – who you really are. Work that out, and you've made a huge leap towards sustainable progress and motivation (more on desire in Part Two).

3. *Set specific goals.* Goals need to be measurable. Too often, our goals are vague – partly because our fear of disappointment has prevented us thinking too hard about the specifics. Stating you want to become an architect or lawyer with your own practice or partnership (perhaps specializing in housing or human rights), when you inwardly feel incapable of such achievements, feels like setting yourself up for failure. So you avoid making such detailed commitments. Yet the opposite is true. By adding detail to your goals you're developing a clear understanding of what has to be achieved. This can be converted into a series of small, achievable steps or milestones that keep you motivated and on-track towards your objectives. Vague goals, meanwhile, will produce only vague directions that fail to motivate. Like driving in the dark, without the clarity offered by strong headlights, you'll simply want to stop.
4. *Visualize your goals.* Detail is important when it comes to goals, even if the details change as you progress. And detail comes not just from drafting plans or researching specifics (though both count) but from imagining your future. What does your future look like? No, I mean *really* look like: office/studio, colleagues and work-projects – as well as your house, car, partner, bedroom, bathroom, garden and dog? Find somewhere quiet, close your eyes, and project yourself forward. Such a vision shouldn't frustrate you. It should motivate you, although not by fantasizing some wildest dream. You need to home in on the minutia of your idealized future, but also ensure it chimes with your values (otherwise it's just fantasizing). Importantly, you should add a timeframe for your visualization that's far enough ahead to plan and execute significant changes. Perhaps ten years should be the minimum – a realistic and fathomable timeframe, though still time enough to allow a total turnaround in your life.
5. *Develop milestones.* Of course, ten years can seem too remote to be immediately motivating. So, with the same level of detail, you should set milestone goals that punctuate the

distance between now and your ten-year objectives. Working backwards, start with five-years – visualizing what *has* to be in place to make the ten-year goal a certainty. Then two years, one year, six months, three months, one month and even one week. Each milestone needs clarity and detail – ensuring that, by the end of the exercise, we have clearly connected points along a path plotting the journey between your current status and ultimate destination. Such a path should also make the next step obvious, which is an important driver for your motivation as it reduces your doubts. One trap to avoid is worrying about the 'how' for a milestone three or four years' hence. Such thoughts can sabotage your goal-setting by generating instant mental limits, which are no more than a self-fulfilling invention. Only for the next small step (the one-week goal perhaps) is there any need to focus on the 'how'.

6. *Write down your goals.* We wonder why others get ahead while we seem stuck. Yet the difference is often that they've written their goals while we possess little more than vague dreams or the odd scribbled note. Written goals are maps, and maps are vital for giving us direction. It couldn't be more obvious: tell two friends to find a remote hamlet while giving only one a map – the one with the map will get there directly, while the one without will simply get lost. So, why's this a step so few people take? To reach any destination we need accurate co-ordinates. And written goals are those co-ordinates.
7. *Reward yourself.* You should view the one-year and other milestones as key points in your journey – as energizing confirmation you're heading in the right direction. This should be reward enough, of course. But why not add some icing on the cake? This doesn't mean indulging yourself in your previously disabling behaviours (see Part Two). But it can mean a small treat such as dinner at a favourite restaurant, a small vacation or some other moment that allows you to breathe in the sweet air of accomplishment. It may also help you reconnect with others, perhaps feeling slightly abandoned by your new

pursuits (see Part Four). Certainly, marking your progress is important if it's to change your attitude and maintain your motivation – although beware the 'you've earned it' indulgence in the very habits that killed your past progress.

## Finding flow

Goals are therefore vital, which is – of course – an easy thing to write. Becoming goal-oriented means changing behaviours that have reinforced your poor productivity over many years, which is why you need to return to your emotions as drivers. And this means revisiting Daniel Goleman's important work on emotional intelligence.

In both *Emotional Intelligence* and his follow up book *Working with Emotional Intelligence* (1998) Goleman cites examples of people who are not only productive but at their peak of productivity: giving everything with every fibre of their being focused and engaged on their productive pursuits.

For instance, he quotes a composer describing the mental zone in which he's most creative:

'You yourself are in an ecstatic state to such a point that you feel as though you almost don't exist. I've experienced this time and again. My hand seems devoid of myself, and I have nothing to do with what is happening. I just sit there watching in a state of awe and wonderment. And it just flows out of itself.'

And while Goleman cites musicians and athletes and chess champions, he also cites engineers and filing clerks and, in *Working with Emotional Intelligence*, a railroad welder called Joe who, after 40 years fixing every machine at his depot in Chicago, still finds his work exhilarating.

'The key to that exhilaration is not the task itself', writes Goleman. 'Joe's job is often routine – but the special state of mind Joe creates as he works, a state called "flow." Flow moves people to do their best work, no matter what work they do.'

When our skills are fully engaged; when we're stretched and challenged but remain confident of progress; when we're concentrating so hard we're unaware of the distractions around us; and when we're nimbly moving between tasks or handling equipment with agility and dexterity – almost without thinking about it: that's 'flow'.

## Flow is a pleasure

With flow, there's no need for motivation, says Goleman. It's built in. Our fears are forgotten, our disappointments history, our creativity unleashed.

'Flow itself is a pleasure', he writes, while 'the work is a delight in itself'.

And, in what Goleman calls a 'neural paradox', he writes of the fact flow involves performing the most demanding tasks while expending the minimal mental energy. It just seems to happen. Meanwhile, when we're bored or apathetic, the brain is an exhausting frenzy of poorly focused activity with 'brain cells firing in far-flung and irrelevant ways'.

'But during flow, the brain appears efficient and precise in its pattern of firing', concludes Goleman.

Flow is one of those concepts I wish I'd been aware of all my life. Certainly, I can look back and recall what caused flow and what didn't: maths (no), essay writing (yes), building surveying (no), history (yes), journalism (yes), banking (no). But to have known that flow was my path to fulfilment, my beam of light – and to plan my route accordingly – would have prevented nearly all of those damaging career diversions and dead ends.

Sure, we may need time to calculate what generates our personal flow and what doesn't – and this is certainly no treatise for an early surrender when finding something difficult. As adults, however, we should have enough experience to discern what can get us into that wonderful state, as well as how we may be able to engage those skills profitably. And, if not, then we now know where we need to start: by looking for what, within us, is capable of generating flow.

## Encouraging flow

But is there anything we can do to encourage flow – any habits we can adopt and changes we can make? In my view, yes. As someone that experiences flow regularly, but has also too much experience of the apathy at the other end of the spectrum, I can outline my own experiences:

- *Open your mind to flow.* Attitude is half the battle. If you want to find flow, you can. If you don't, you won't. If you don't look for it, or if you assume it's not going to happen, your disinterest or disbelief will be self-fulfilling.
- *Focus on (or find) your talents:* Flow doesn't emerge from the formalized work that your parents or seniors have forced upon you. It comes from what you're good at. And, if you think you're not good at anything, then you must realize that your destructive self-beliefs have been lying to you (not for the first time). We're all good at *something* – focus on that (or focus on finding it) and worry about its profitability later (more on this in Part Two).
- *Be motivated.* In fact there's no need to write this – if you're good at something, you'll love doing it, which will give you all the motivation you need. Ignore any dissenting voices telling you what you should and shouldn't be doing. It's your life. It's the only one you'll get. And no one else is going to live it for you. So spend it doing something you love. If you do, you'll find flow. Not only that, once you've found flow the world will conspire on your behalf.
- *Set challenging goals.* While you should always focus on the immediate next steps, and concern yourself with achieving them, such steps must lead you somewhere you want to go. I

mean *really* want to go. Flow comes from having direction – building your confidence step-by-step as we move towards truly motivational goals. This is no time to short-change yourself with a 'reality check'. Be bold. If you're pursuing your talents you'll find a way of making it sustainable.

- *Reduce your leisure time.* Studies at the University of Chicago (analyzing flow) found that the most common emotional state recorded during leisure time was apathy. This is a dangerous state because it can quickly feel normal, meaning we cannot motivate ourselves to restart work. If you're now motivated to do what you love – cut out the TV (or pub or golf course) and do it!
- *Kill destructive behaviour.* In fact, don't stop at killing TV time. Playing games with your blood-sugar levels through too much alcohol or from a poor diet can also lead to apathy. You must take responsibility for your physical as well as mental state and realize that neglect in one area feeds neglect elsewhere. Believe in self-improvement – starting with better habits. I cycle to work, I use the gym every workday, I gave up smoking and alcohol, I never take drugs, I reduced the amount of fat in my diet. Every single one of these moves has incrementally improved my ability to find flow (more on habits in Part Two).
- *Focus on one task – removing all other distractions.* Multi-tasking is the death of flow. You need a laser-like focus on one task. My task now is to finish this chapter. But I also need to call a client, chase a payment and prepare for a midday meeting. Yet I'm reading these tasks from a to-do list in front of me (more on to-do lists in Part Two). I'll get to them – sure – but my only focus *now* is on finishing this chapter. Nothing else matters.
- *Create a sense of urgency.* This is an interesting one because most self-help literature talks about reducing stress. Of course, too much stress is counterproductive but – if you've set yourself time-based milestones to achieve your goals – you need to meet them. Urgency matters. You've spent too much time in an unproductive state – while others have motored ahead due to

their focus. Well here's where you start catching up, so there's no time to lose. Goleman writes about good stress – when the adrenalin flows and the brain is attentive, interested and energized. Time pressure can generate that adrenalin *rush* so – within reason – you should let it.

- *Record your progress.* You have to sustain this behaviour over a long period (in fact the rest of your life), not just a week or so while its novel. And the best way to reinforce your progress is by writing it down. I use an A5 page-per-day diary with my ten-year goals stated at the back (in the 'notes' pages), along with my milestones. Meanwhile, my journey towards them is recorded daily. I also record my feelings at the time – even apathy – and my progress towards controlling destructive behaviour. It doesn't always work – I occasionally fall off the wagon (usually with food) or become overly self-condemning after a setback. But recording this also helps me rationalize it and, importantly, move on. I'm soon back on track, after writing down the lessons – and plotting a new path in my diary.

**Get Things Done:** *Your disabling self-beliefs have perpetuated your malaise. Unfortunately, no one is coming to your rescue. But, with strong motivation – created from strong goals and good planning – you can develop the 'flow' and self-control required to make strong progress.*

# PART TWO

# Tools and Resources

# 5
# THE NEED FOR DESIRE

In 1937, Napoleon Hill published *Think and Grow Rich*, his famous work on the 13 steps required for generating vast personal wealth. The book built on his 20-year exploration of the character traits of America's richest self-made industrialists, which resulted in his first book, *Law of Success* (1928). This work took eight volumes and 1,500 pages to extol the 17 principles for high achievement gleaned from interviewing 500 of the country's most successful people.

Yet, despite Hill's volumes, his formulaic discoveries became ultimately distilled into four crucial elements. These are, he claimed, desire, faith, plans and persistence.

Of course, these need to be in the right order. After all, persistence prior to plans may result in wasted endeavour, and plans are pointless unless we first have faith they can be executed. Nonetheless, this simple formula should be borne in mind for anyone seeking success, says Hill – or for that matter productivity where there was once unproductive mental chaos.

Intriguingly, Hill also alluded to a 'great universal truth' – a 'supreme secret' that underpins the 17 principles or 13 steps, and even the four elements of his distillation. His patron, Andrew Carnegie (the Scottish-American steel magnate), apparently confirmed this mysterious ingredient in the elixir of success, although it was written down only in 1967, shortly before Hill's death.

Here it is:

'Anything the human mind can believe, the human mind can achieve.'

That's it! There are no limits to what we can achieve, Hill intonates, other than those we impose on ourselves due to our limiting self-beliefs. Those that accept this – truly, fully, unambiguously – will 'think and grow rich' or achieve other extraordinary feats (Hill was as impressed by Ghandi as he was by Carnegie, Ford, Woolworth and Gillette). Meanwhile, the rest of us will struggle – generating the very barriers that we assumed were hindering our progress.

Oh dear.

For me (and others like me) this feels immediately condemning. As stated, self-belief has been my biggest failing – meaning I've behaved in ways that generate the very failure I feared. I even manage to conjure a self-fulfilling defeat from the jaws of victory simply because, beneath it all, I've no faith that a successful outcome is possible.

## Desire – the starting point of all achievement

Yet Hill's formula offers another potential clue as to why my efforts had been so fruitless: I'd disobeyed his sequencing. As stated, plans without faith will fail despite persistence. So – just maybe – the key missing ingredient for generating faith is what Hill insists is 'the starting point of all achievement: desire'. Would I develop the faith that allowed me to persist with my plans if I could conjure sufficient desire?

In fact, I can immediately confirm this to be true. Ultimately, I've not failed. Here I am, writing my fourth book, with only the first (a 'lad-lit' comedy about my time in New York) deemed a failure by any measure (and even that was a largely self-imposed assessment). However modestly, my writing has succeeded to the point it's converted my directionless and ultimately unproductive frustrations into a fulfilling and sustainable path. Why? Because writing is my *thing*; and being a writer is what I've always desired. Anything else – surveying, banking, entrepreneurship – always felt like a replacement activity for my ultimate desire, which was to write.

What's more, this desire has resulted in a strong belief in my writing. In fact, it's the one area of my life where I've maintained strong self-belief no matter what the setbacks or criticisms. Sure, my first book flopped (by my measure) but I've never doubted my writing skills: just that the book was poorly marketed or that my publisher erroneously failed to share my faith in the book's excellence.

Having made writing the core of my existence, therefore, I've succeeded. My desire to write gave me faith, which led to strong planning and dogged persistence – confirming the veracity of Hill's distilled process.

And if it works for me – believe me – it can work for others.

The key is to understand Hill's core message, which is that – while plans are important – they're impossible to fulfil without faith. And faith relies on desire. Only once we've discovered *the* pursuit, where we believe in our skills – our *thing* – will we develop both the flow and stoicism required to make serious progress. And, if we're struggling to find *the* thing, it maybe because we've been looking in the wrong place. Perhaps due to external pressures we've been sent down the wrong path – told to pursue careers or skills that, deep down, we don't desire.

Hill and Carnegie's supreme secret, therefore, is as much to do with desire as it is with belief, because only desire can generate that level of belief. Desire comes first – so that's where we must start our journey towards successful productivity.

## Definiteness of purpose

In his section on desire, Hill tells the story of Edwin C. Barnes, whose greatest desire was to be the business partner of renowned inventor Thomas Edison (he of light-bulb fame). In fact, all Barnes possessed was desire – he had no qualifications and not even the train fare for the journey to Edison's New Jersey yard (arriving hobo-style on a freight train). Yet, eventually, that's exactly what happened. Barnes became Edison's partner to market the Ediphone (an early dictation device).

Barnes succeeded because his desire was focused on a single pursuit that absorbed all his energy and willpower. He was also persistent – working menially in Edison's workshop for years prior to seeing his chance via a product others dismissed as a likely flop.

'It is a remarkable illustration of the power of a definite desire', writes Hill. 'Barnes won his goal, because he wanted to be a business associate of Mr Edison, more than he wanted anything else.'

Of course, this can all sound a bit old-fashioned to modern ears – a bit like the admonishments of our elders and betters. But the tone isn't meant to be hectoring. It's meant to point out that – if we're demotivated and even a little listless – it may be because we've yet to find, or yet to find a way of profitably pursuing, what we truly desire.

## Growing a vocation

Modern writers make exactly the same point as Hill, although are less focused on wealth or material desires and more on what could be termed 'meaning'.

'I regularly hear people lament that they are "still searching for their vocation" or envying others who have "found their ultimate calling,"' writes School of Life co-founder Roman Krznaric in his 2012 book *How to Find Fulfilling Work*. 'What they seem to be looking for is a career that offers them an all-embracing sense of mission or purpose.'

That said, Krznaric is cautious about the notion of searching for *the* thing: a vocation that jumps out and declares itself so, 'not because vocations do not exist', he writes, 'but because we have to realize that a vocation is not something we *find*, it's something we *grow* – and grow into.'

Those striving for their vocation often remain frustrated, says Krznaric, because they spend too much time looking for *the thing* they were 'meant to do'. Yet such a search may be too great a leap, he claims. Instead, they should pursue a career that motivates them 'to get up in the morning', from which will emerge the goal that gives their work meaning.

'The goal or purpose of the medical researcher might be to discover a cure for motor neurone disease', says Krznaric. 'For an environmental activist it could be to promote the ideal of low-carbon living, for a painter, to break traditional conventions and replace them with a new vision of the objectives of art.'

In all cases, their purpose emerged from within careers that motivated them – a concept I can confirm. Via journalism, public relations and now, authoring, I've established that writing is my *thing*. But only slowly has my vocation emerged – of combining my writing and PR skills to articulate what I've learnt about my own insecurities.

These insecurities always held me back, as they do for millions. Yet I never lost my desire to write, or my faith that my writing is worth reading. Just that I lacked the opportunity, or the self-belief, to push myself forwards. Finally, the penny dropped regarding the roots of my issues and, suddenly, my skills and desires were aligned to create my vocation, which quickly translated into strong plans, persistence, and sustainable progress.

Meaning emerged from following my desire to write, and allowing that to gel into a specific – and life-changing – goal.

## Suffering's meaning

A further perspective on this comes from Viktor Frankl, a Viennese psychiatrist specializing in depression. In 1944, his entire family was transported to the Nazi death camp Auschwitz, with only

Viktor and his sister surviving to tell the tale. And tell the tale he did: the experience acted as the catalyst for his famous 1946 work *Man's Search for Meaning*.

Frankl wrote what I consider to be a tremendously important statement for the insecure, under-confident or simply ineffective person trying to turn their life in a positive direction: 'suffering ceases to be suffering', he said, 'at the moment it finds a meaning.'

In other words, we can use our suffering – even our ineffectiveness – as fuel for achieving higher things, which gives our pain purpose.

In the camps, Frankl discovered what he called the 'last of the human freedoms', which was his attitude. He had the freedom to choose the mental impact his imprisonment would have on him which, extraordinarily, made him freer than his Nazi captors.

He decided he would use his experiences to lecture the world on the human condition as he saw it, a visualization that sustained him through the horror and gave him the will to survive. Indeed, Frankl's suffering ceased the moment he saw that it had meaning – that there was a higher purpose.

## Finding faith

Next comes faith. We have to believe that we can achieve what we desire or our quest is doomed, considers Hill.

'In faith is the "external elixir" which gives life, power, and action to the impulse of thought', writes Hill. 'Faith is the starting point of all accumulation of riches . . . [and is] the basis of all "miracles."'

This is far from a religious quest, although it can feel just as abstract to those who lack self-belief. Indeed, Hill doesn't deny the difficulty of injecting or even expressing faith or self-belief into those that lack it: like describing 'the colour red to a blind man who's never seen colour' was how he termed it. That said, he considered it a state of mind that could be developed – oddly through the process of repetition.

'Repetition of affirmation of orders to your subconscious mind is the only known method of voluntary development of the emotion of faith', he writes.

Hill is a rational thinker aware that such statements may come across as too mystical for his audience of ambitious rationalists. He therefore used studies in criminology to prove his point.

'When men first come into contact with crime, they abhor it', he claimed (quoting an unnamed criminologist). 'If they remain in contact with crime for a time, they become accustomed to it, and endure it. If they remain in contact with it long enough, they finally embrace it, and become influenced by it.'

By the same measure, Hill claims that any thought that's repeatedly invoked within us will become part of our subconscious mind and therefore accepted and translated into an impulse to act. And that includes faith.

Again, this may hit the brick wall of our inbuilt cynicism, constructed from years of setbacks and frustrations. In fact, we may even see cynicism as an intelligent response. Who, after all, wants to be the willing pawn of those trying to manipulate us, perhaps through pedalling faith?

Yet, two points tell me that we *can* develop the self-belief we need to succeed. First is the fact that many of us have developed strong convictions regarding our failures or inabilities. Sure, we may feel these are evidence-based, but they're convictions nonetheless; just negative ones. Our need is therefore not to develop faith (which we patently have), but to develop faith in our positive aspirations (or even, as stated, our plans), rather than our negative (self-perceived) attributes.

And, second, is the fact that what we seek is not a spiritual or religious rebirth. There's nothing supernatural going on here – just the notion that faith cannot be bluffed or conjured from thin air. It has to be *real* faith. But – importantly – it doesn't have to be *total* faith.

As stated, this isn't religious. We require the faith to act, and to keep acting through the setbacks. That's all. Our poor faith currently stalls our progress. Yet we simply need a tipping point – where the weight of our faith rebalances in favour of action, and against procrastination.

## Looking for the nugget

The aim here is not to lie to yourself. You just need to convince yourself of the truth, which makes the place to start the journey towards faith that one nugget – the single thing you're good at no matter how deep and broad your other deficiencies. If nothing else, you can surely develop faith in one attribute or talent (in my case, writing). This is your redoubt – the faith you maintain no matter what the criticism of others, or even in spite of the self-critic within. In your deepest self you know this is something you can do well. No matter how small a thing it is – or how pathetic and useless you feel it to be – this *thing* can be the seed that propagates your inner faith.

Of course, faith has to be expanded – not least into something offering a sustainable future. And it also has to connect back to desire: you have to grow your faith around something you want. Yet, in my opinion, that's the easy bit. Almost certainly, your talents have followed your desires, not least because – as we've seen – this generates flow. So your only need is to plan a sustainable future using that talent – not least because that's where you've invested your faith.

This brings us back to our plans, and our need to believe in them, which we'll develop below. Yet we still have to conquer those lingering doubts – perhaps that our talent-base is too small or too irrelevant to develop into a profitable pursuit.

In fact, such thoughts make me angry – not with the sufferer, I hasten to add, who I consider a victim despite their apparent lack of attributes (which many will assume makes their low status somehow deserved). But with their education. If we reach adulthood feeling useless it's almost certainly due to poor education – whether this came about via our family or within a formalized structure such as a national education system. We've been failed by them because they didn't spot our talents or didn't know how to develop them.

This is an outrageous crime, in my opinion. But one which, guided by Viktor Frankl's philosophy of developing meaning from suffering, we must turn to our advantage in adulthood. Such a poor start will give our progress real purpose: personally, spiritually and, hopefully, sustainably.

Are we too late? Not if we have sufficient desire. If we do, it's never too late – as long as we can muster the faith to get going.

An example to illustrate: a previous girlfriend of mine declared herself a 'bit thick'. Despite its frustrations, she clung to a low-level sales job that leveraged her good looks – assuming she was incapable of anything more cerebral. During one less-than-thrilling evening, however, we started playing *Connect Four* (the logic game involving placing coloured discs in a row while trying to block an opponent). She thrashed me. Game after game, I was no match due to her ability to spot emerging patterns and opportunities as the game progressed.

Over several sessions, this proved to be no fluke: she was definitely a whizz at *Connect Four*. We then tried chess, which she'd never played. By the second game I was, again, relegated to the role of enthusiastic loser. She had an eye for sequences of moves and their consequences that left me for dead.

Of course, such skills have to be bankable, although a little thinking would soon sort that out. Sure, becoming a chess pro may have seemed a (self-imposed) stretch for an Essex girl (although a beautiful blond chess champion would have certainly been noticed). Yet it was obvious she could analyze possible strategies, plan outcomes, remove choices, integrate changes – even calculate algorithms: all attributes employable in careers well above what she saw as her lowly role flogging beauty products.

Alas, my ex-girlfriend didn't desire a career in management consultancy or as an analyst or strategist, although – in my opinion – this was due to her poor education. She'd left school with nothing more than low confidence and a conviction that professional careers were not for the likes of her. If she'd developed faith from her desires, however, the outcome could have been very different.

**Get Things Done:** *Desire, faith, plans and persistence are the key requirements for success. Yet these have to be achieved in the right order, meaning we can only develop faith in something we desire, which is usually our thing. This may be something we have to develop over time, although we don't need total faith – just enough to act.*

# 6

# PLANNING FOR FREEDOM

Plans are the easy bit. Honest. Execution is the difficult bit; and even that's a lot easier with some strong planning. Also, notice what's happened here: an easy bit of planning has eased us into some doable execution – and on we go until the next bit of required planning. Too often we try to kickstart our endeavours with some frantic activity, which relies on our willpower to keep going. Willpower that soon collides with a small setback – or interruption – and disappears, almost as quickly as it's conjured.

Instead, we should kick-start our new endeavours, not with frantic activity – or 'busy-ness' as Stephen Covey calls it in *7 Habits of Highly Effective People* (1989) – but with manic planning. And if we get distracted after 10 minutes – so what? We've had a good 10-minute planning session that we can build upon (as long as we've written it down). In fact, after 10 minutes we *should* do something else, and then come back and check that our plans still make sense.

Of course, in our enthusiasm, we may have written nonsense. Yet this is nothing to beat ourselves up about: nonsensical plans are a good start, as long as they're replaced at some point with executable ones. As a writer, I know that first drafts are far more important than perfect first drafts (which don't exist). Even terrible first drafts are a strong document to work from: a start, a structure, as well as some text that can be reorganized and rewritten.

If nothing else, we've managed to eliminate an unworkable idea. The process of unravelling or capturing thoughts and ideas, and placing them in the correct order using the right language, has begun.

The same goes for planning: bad ideas are great because they're a step towards good ideas that we can execute.

If our plans are *not* nonsense, however, we can spend another 10 minutes adding some flesh. In fact, this may be an effective work pattern in the early stages: 10 minutes of intense thinking (not action) and writing (or sketching), followed by a short break or (not too diverting) alternative activity, followed by a further 10 minutes of concentrated work.

Indeed, why not actually time it – perhaps using one of those alarmed kitchen timers?

## The Pomodoro Technique

No, I didn't invent this. It's called the Pomodoro Technique and it's a favourite of time managers the world over, although the brainchild of Italian Francesco Cirillo.

Named after those tomato-shaped devices used in most Italian kitchens, the Pomodoro Technique breaks all activities into intense work sessions of no more than 25 minutes followed by a break. Yet we're happy to make it 10 minutes because we're planning, which is more thinking than doing so therefore more mentally taxing.

This immediately generates a strong and doable work rhythm. In Cirillo's view, the very act of winding-up the timer creates an urgency that triggers action, as does the gentle whirring or ticking and the impending alarm. For the disorganized person the technique establishes the relationship between time and activity – creating an intensity of concentration and an intolerance of interruptions (as well as a time-zone for allowable interruptions). And why stop with the work? Why not time the break the same way – making resetting the alarm our first and last action during the 10-minute work period?

Cirillo also suggests a low-tech approach, at least at first. In his view (and mine) early planning stages should be scribbled using pen and paper. Perhaps a later 10-minute session can convert the paper notes into an electronic format, although this should be seen as part of the editing process. For now, uninterrupted thought is the key requirement so anything that potentially distracts us – including electrons emitting from a screen (thus straining our eyes) – should be avoided.

## The rhythm of process

In fact this rhythm – in this case 10 minutes on, 10 minutes off, 10 minutes on again – is an important concept because such rhythms run right through any universe focused on getting things done. Disorganized and unproductive people are simply those that miss the upbeat of the rhythm. We start, we break, we start again: with the second uptake of work often the problematic point for the inattentive or distracted person.

Well here's a reminder to restart work which, even if we do 10-minutes on and 20 off, still means 20 minutes of intense work each hour, or nearly three hours per working day: enough to get anyone well on the road to strong productivity (although the aim should be to slowly expand the up-time to Cirillo's 25-minute preference).

In my view, Cirillo's simple contribution is immediately transforming – recruiting both unproductive time and disorganization to our cause because they now have their place, which mirrors the rhythm of our lives.

'One reason why people resist getting organized is that they think it is a static condition', writes Dr Marilyn Paul in *Why Am I So Disorganised?*

By this, Paul means that being disorganized is just another part of productivity. At the right moment we simply need to use it as a lever to swing on to the next stage – a process Paul describes thus:

- being ready for action, leads to . . .
- action, which ultimately generates . . .
- natural disorder, which requires . . .
- a restoration of order and habits to make us . . .
- ready for action.

A battle analogy is perhaps the easiest to visualize. Neat ranks of soldiers engage with the enemy and, before long, the battlefield is a ragged and messy place. Yet with the battle over the ranks can reform, march back to barracks, rest, and then ready themselves for the next engagement. And if a war analogy is not to our taste we can think of team sports that begin with neat formations that dissolve into chaos, requiring the periodic restoration of order as the game proceeds.

Of course, it's that restoration that troubles the unproductive mind, although it's a natural part of the rhythm: just the next step. Desks get messy, our creativity dissipates and projects go off on tangents. So we need to ensure we periodically restore order – perhaps a task for the last pomodoro session of the morning.

## So how, and what, do we plan?

With a working rhythm established, and the need for planning understood, the obvious next step is to write (or at this stage sketch/scribble) some plans. Yet we need to be aware that plans can be disabling documents for the unproductive person. The last thing we should create is a mental prison from which we immediately want to escape. Indeed, this feels like a catch-22 situation when it comes to planning: we need plans to become productive but plans are the very thing unproductive people rebel against.

How do we get beyond this? Not easy, given the self-sabotaging thought process we're likely to have adopted thus far. Yet we clearly recognize that such poor thinking has betrayed us, which should put us in the right frame of mind – as long as we can tailor planning to our individual style.

That said, we must first accept certain truths about planning.

1. *Recognize that nothing is set in stone.* Plans are working documents, no more. There's nothing final about a plan. In fact, finalized plans can be too brittle, meaning they'll break when put under pressure. Sure, they should be detailed. But that's to get us thinking and to act as a guide for our actions. There's nothing holy about the text – far from it.
2. *Plans are our servants, not our masters.* They're there to help – guiding us through the mental maze of turning desires into actions. The point is to liberate us from the energy-sapping tyranny of wasted endeavour, not to forge a pair of intellectual handcuffs.
3. *Plans can be tailored to our own working style.* Indeed, this is vital. Plans that jar with our personalities will feel like an imposition. That said, this may be a question of our habits, which may need to change (see below). But it may be more fundamental – perhaps forcing a scientific or analytical approach on someone more creative and emotional. Again, such a clash may explain our current dysfunction, which makes our new plans an opportunity to put this right. Fail to do so here and the malaise continues: with, again, small setbacks or disruptions derailing our productivity.
4. *Plans should set no hard-and-fast deadlines.* Rather, plans should simply be a thought-through path towards a completion point that we decide for ourselves. That's not a moment in time but a visualized place or completed project. Although it may suit our purpose to state time-based expectations, they're a guide to help draw the path, not an axe poised to fall at a particular moment. Indeed, the invented deadlines of others can

be the thing we most hate – so it would be madness to invent and impose our own.

5. *The perfect plan does not exist.* In fact, if we think we've written one we may simply have failed to discover the flaws. So we should not look for perfection or become angry with the obvious flaws in our current draft. They're simply wrinkles that can be ironed out as we get to them. Of course, detail is important. But so is flexibility. Plans are to get us going and retain our momentum. Insisting on the perfect plan, therefore, may be nothing more than a tactic for avoiding execution (the classic ruse of the procrastinator).

## Begin with the end in mind

So, what should our planning include? Well this is where we start our journey, so our key need is a destination. Stephen Covey made his second habit 'begin with the end in mind' which, I think, is a worthy starting point for any planning. His first habit, by the way, was 'be proactive', which should, by now, be well understood. It's the direction of our proactivity we're trying to establish.

'To begin with the end in mind means to start with a clear understanding of your destination', writes Covey. 'It means to know where you're going so that you better understand where you are now and so that the steps you take are always in the right direction.'

Covey states that it's easy to get caught in the 'activity trap', in which we work harder and harder to climb a ladder that's leaning against the wrong wall.

'It's possible to be busy – very busy – without being effective', he states, invoking the vision of explorers cutting their way through the jungle towards their stated goal only for the leader to climb the tallest tree, survey the terrain, and shout down: 'wrong jungle!'

'Shut up!' others reply, 'we're making progress.'

Our primary planning exercise, therefore, requires us to find the right jungle. In itself, this may be a difficult endeavour given the unproductive person's propensity for self-sabotage and avoidance. Indeed, our core aims – at this stage – may be purely negative: of not wanting something (conformity perhaps), rather than wanting something.

Yet, given a turnaround in thinking, even this situation can open up positive possibilities. We simply need to reframe the language.

For instance, if we examine the negative and rebellious statement 'I don't want to conform', we could reframe it to the more positive 'I want to express myself freely'. This means we've immediately generated a framework that has the 'end in mind': we want to do our own thing.

Then, if we look at what we're good at or what we like (utilizing Hill's notion of desire) – art, maths, IT or English (for example) – we can perhaps add to the statement: 'I want to express myself freely in art/maths/IT/English etc.'

This certainly gives us something positive to work towards. Going back to my own chaotic youth this would probably have been English, given that I loved writing essays. So, taking this exercise to its conclusion: my first pomodoro planning session would have concluded with the statement: 'I want to express myself freely in writing English', which should lead me to think about the possible avenues for making that desire a reality. These include becoming a novelist, script writer or a journalist – perhaps choosing journalism because it offers a strong training and opens the door to further, even freer, literary expression later on.

All of a sudden, I've a 10-year goal – not to become a journalist (that's a mere milestone), but to express myself freely as a writer: perhaps writing feature articles or commentaries, or even branching out into TV documentaries or non-fiction books. *Wow!* That's one hell of an end result – and one easily conjured from the mere reversal of our negatively framed urges.

Such reframing is an easy exercise and one we should all undertake, no matter where the negativity lies or how far along a particular career path we've travelled. It's also a great first action on our journey towards productivity – not least because it marks a major moment of transition between the id and the ego of Freud's early organizational impulses, as well as between negative and positive thinking and between unproductive and productive endeavour.

## Beyond the desired end result

But what then? Getting beyond the desired end result can be a painful process, because the more detail we add the more it feels like our warm, soft, fluffy desires are coming up against the cold hard rocks of reality. Yet it's way too soon for such catastrophic thinking – not least because it's probably the result of too little planning.

Becoming over-enthused by one idea, and then headlessly charging forth is the quickest and most needless way to slam against those rocks of reality. Needless, because stronger planning, and a greater calculation of future actions, would have shown us how to deftly navigate such barriers.

According to David Allen, in his influential book *Getting Things Done* (2001), there are five phases to what he calls 'natural planning', although – in our Covey-inspired enthusiasm – we've somewhat corrupted his process.

These are (with some thoughts of my own):

1. *Defining your purpose and principles*. This is all about motivating ourselves to act, which of course is important. We should therefore be comfortable we've got to this point before we move on to the next stage. It never hurts to ask the 'why' question, says Allen. And your prime criteria for action should be your values and principles, which agrees with Stephen Covey and just about everyone else I've read on this.

2. *Outcome visioning.* Visualization is such a strong technique that it's worth repeating: in my own case perhaps visualizing the writer in 'flow', hunched over a keyboard with shelves of books behind me (some of which I've written!) and the notes for my next endeavour stacked up on my desk. And there's no harm going further: my desk, the view out of the window, the dog at my feet, the kids in the garden. Details are important for envisioned outcomes. So don't be too embarrassed: not only to think them but to write them down (your plan is a deeply private document, don't forget, so you're free to indulge your fantasies).
3. *Brainstorming.* This is about identifying all the elements of our project – not, at this stage, in any particular order. Mind mapping may help to calculate the entirety of what's required (see below), although I can find myself more fascinated by the patterns than the ideas, so I'm equally happy with lists (as is Allen). Certainly, once in 'flow' the ideas should come quickly, and can be judged later for their quality in the 'organizing' process.
4. 'Once you perceive a basic structure, your mind will start trying to fill in the blanks', says Allen. 'Identifying three key things that you need to handle on the project, for example, may cause you to think of a fourth and a fifth when you see them all lined up'.
5. *Organizing.* Having identified the significant elements of our project we need to sort them into priorities and processes. What must happen to generate the end result, and in what order? What's vital, what's important, what's desirable but not crucial? Hierarchy is critical here, as is sequencing.
6. *Next actions.* At this point I always imagine a funnel. We've poured everything in but what comes out should be a sequence of one-by-one executable actions. Projects are a linear process – only manageable if we plot our progress via a series of small, doable next steps.

'Consistently managing your next action for each [project] will constitute 90 percent of what's generally thought of as project planning', says Allen.

Next actions are therefore a key outcome of planning, although – please note – this is the last element of planning once we've corralled all the elements we need. It's also the first time we should add the word 'how' to our thinking – although only for the first action along what is now a linear and sequential to-do list.

## Mind mapping

For me, the most troubling element of the above is brainstorming. This is what Allen calls the 'how' mechanism, although focusing on how something is to be achieved can be immediately disabling. Our poor self-beliefs may generate fear and doubt the instant we try to calculate executable paths for our goals. Yet Allen isn't suggesting we rationalize our thoughts into doable actions (at least, not yet) – just that we come up with options: as many options in as many directions as we can muster (again, we'll edit them later).

Mind mapping is Allen's preferred visual aid for brainstorming. Coined by British psychology author, Tony Buzan, this popular method results in a spider-like graph with the core notion at the centre and with limbs going in all directions – spouting their own legs as ideas proliferate.

The example Allen uses is of a project to move offices. The stated aim is circled in the centre of the page, with major limbs given labels such as 'timing', 'budget', 'location' and 'address changes'. Subsidiary branches develop the supplementary thoughts these produce. For instance, on the 'address changes' branch Allen includes 'new stationery', 'business cards' and 'notifying clients' – all thoughts taking the project an executable stage further on from the original 'move office' objective.

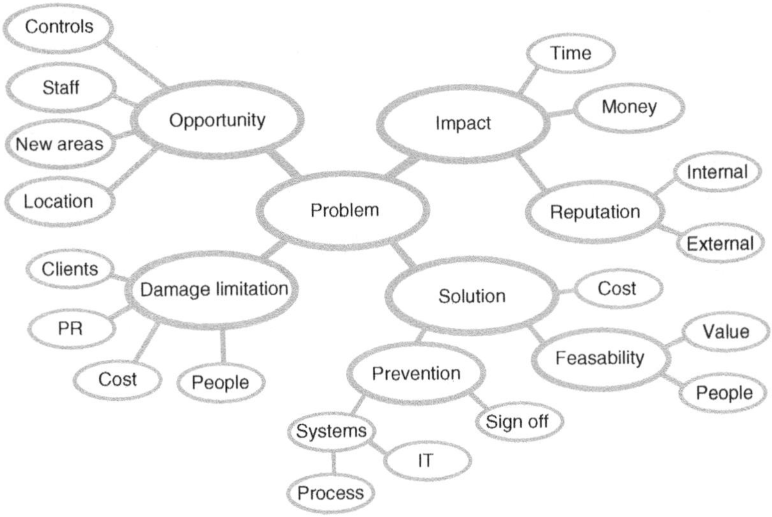


**Figure 2** A mindmap showing a typical office 'problem' generating subsidiary concerns

To me, mind maps are no more than a good starting point – helping us capture and structure random thoughts and perhaps unblock constrained or problem-seeking thinking. To become useful for execution, however, mind maps need to become a written-up action plan under various headings.

But that's just my view. Others may love the visual and spatial freedom they provide – like an explosion of thought that still manages to record sequences and actions, perhaps on its outer edges, like stars in an expanding universe.

A final thing to remember about brainstorming: it's *not* creative thinking, which may be a later part of the process. Sure, brainstorming can aid or promote creative thinking, and most certainly it's inspirational. But its main aim is to generate ideas and concepts that revolve around a specific problem or project. Creativity is therefore no more than a branch of brainstorming, while another branch will be the practicalities of achievement, or timing concerns, or required resources or permissions. As Allen states, the aim of brainstorming is the 'quantity not quality' of thoughts.

> **Get Things Done:** *Proactivity has its own rhythm that we need to adopt, including constructive downtime. The rest is planning, which – at this stage – involves finding the 'right jungle' and brainstorming the entirety of needs, as well as our next actions.*

# 7

# GETTING STARTED

I've always had a weakness for the rule-of-10 writing style. *Top-10 Tips for Beating the Blues*, that sort of thing. Many self-help writers adopt this method – not least because it creates a logical framework for recommended endeavours. Sure, it's often a stretch or a squeeze, meaning it should have been 9 or 11 (or even 8 or 12). But 10 is a recallable number that'll help when trying to keep the tips in mind, so it's worth the nip-and-tuck.

Caveats aside, here are the 10 key points to note when getting started.

## *Point One*: Love your workstation

Your workstation is the cockpit for your journey, so it has to be a place where you want to spend time. If the seat's uncomfortable, or so poorly adjusted it gives you backache or repetitive strain injury, you'll be desperate to leave soon after arriving – meaning you'll almost certainly fail the second Pomodoro session. The same is true of the outlook. If you're having to muse, plan and execute your future by constantly regarding something you dislike – or that distracts you – it'll kill your productivity.

So take time to get it right. Play with the arrangement: desk and chair in this or that corner, facing in or out from the wall, next or away from the window. Also, the desk elements need to aid your progress, not encumber it. So the computer screen position matters, as does the keyboard, mouse, in-trays, files, printer, phone, contacts book and whatever else.

There's no right or wrong way: this isn't an instruction manual. But there'll be a right and wrong way for you, which you should notice and obey. For instance, constantly struggling with the mouse for want of a mousepad (as my wife does), or realizing your contacts book and phone are located at different ends of the desk (as mine were), but doing nothing about it, are mild forms of self-sabotage.

Of course, your workstation also needs to be somewhere you can concentrate, so quietness is another requirement. This is far from easy in the modern house, where architectural trends prefer open-plan spaces; or office, where open-plan work zones are now the norm. At the very least we need somewhere we can block out the distractions, so if we cannot separate ourselves physically then we should invest in a good set of headphones and some suitable mood music to aid concentration. And turn it up LOUD ENOUGH TO BLOCK OUT THE WORLD.

Our workstation is vital – wherever it is and whatever it consists of (the same is true of a workbench). If you don't love it – and I mean *love* it: enjoy its company, admire its look, want to buy it presents – it won't love you back, and the relationship will immediately be off to a bad start.

## *Point Two*: Invest in the right equipment

Of course, the same is true of our equipment. These are the tools of our trade so they need to be an aid to our progress. Cool holidays, designer clothes, posh restaurants, even that morning latte – these are all indulgences. The right equipment is essential and, if that means top-of-the-range, so be it – not least because spending money on the right gear is a strong statement of intent.

By this I don't mean buy the most expensive Mac when you only need a word-processor (although the indulgence may fall into the 'love your workstation' category, which makes it allowable). I'm simply stating that anything that disables or hinders you must be eliminated.

For instance, on many occasions I've struggled with some household DIY – perhaps a plumbing problem – and ultimately had to call in the professionals. They suck their teeth and knowingly shake their heads. But then they unload a piece of specialist kit that's built for the job. Within minutes, they've dealt with my hour-long struggle, and I'm handed a hefty bill (partly because they're still paying for that piece of specialist equipment).

No, having the right kit is not half the battle (only our attitude comes with that much influence). But it's a good 25 percent, which makes it worth our investment.

## *Point Three*: Buy lots of stationery

I love stationery. I write books and I run a PR agency, which means being well-organized – making stationery my specialist equipment.

The right stationery is as cool as sunglasses. I love watching our account directors attend a meeting with a smart notepad and slick pen. It makes such a difference: we concentrate harder, we ask better questions, our eye contact is more assured. Those notebooks say that we're in control – going places. Yes, I am being flippant – but flippancies sometimes matter (especially in the perception-oriented world of PR).

Good stationery – like good equipment – works on many levels. It's not just the love of using it, or what it can do for our organizational needs. It's the message we give ourselves. We're serious. We mean business. We're future oriented. Good stationery is the walking boots of our endeavour; so, again, it's worth the expense.

One last thing on stationery. As previously stated, we must buy and use a diary. No, I don't mean for appointments, although they can be included (and some form of day-to-day organizer is a must). I mean a day-per-page journal where we can record our progress. Where are we on our journey? What's just happened? Why? What's next? What's our best approach? What went right/ wrong? What are the lessons? Who should we call? What should we say?

Diaries are our immediate and future planning document. They're also our record of execution. They're the explosion of thoughts, as well as the filter. Yet they're also unstructured documents (other than the day divisions) so they're not forcing us to be more organized. They demand no rationality or process. They're simply a private, internal conversation. Yet, almost unconsciously, they add rationality to irrationality, strategy to tactics, and future thinking to daily records. Without a diary, productivity goes unnoticed and lessons unlearnt.

## *Point Four*: Gather/capture everything

Having built our cockpit we now need to fill the aircraft. We should give ourselves a few hours to simply collect stuff. Everything: papers, letters, bills, books, brochures, folders, business cards – the lot.

David Allen (2001) states that this is the critical first step to getting things done: 'Corralling your stuff' as he calls it.

'Just gathering a few more things than you currently have will probably create a positive feeling for you', he writes. 'But if you hang in there and really do the whole collection process, 100 percent, it will change your experience dramatically and give you an important new reference point for being on top of your work.'

Even if it seems overwhelming, this is still an important early job. As Allen states, it's helpful to have a sense of the volume.

'It lets you know where the "end of the tunnel" is', he states, as well as eliminating any doubts regarding that hidden to-do list or pile that may be lurking somewhere. Nothing is lurking anywhere – it's all in one big fat pile in front of us!

## *Point Five:* Do some filing

With the skyscraper built, we now have to knock it down, or at least divide it up. Don't worry – this isn't as boring or daunting as it seems, because nothing requires our actions at this stage. We simply need to pay each item some gnat-like attention to consign it to what Allen calls the 'right buckets', although cardboard boxes may be better depository devices, especially if they're A4 (or US Letter) size.

Label the boxes: say, Project A for our key endeavour, Project B for a supplementary endeavour (perhaps a later milestone) and Project C for our home-personal life – any more boxes than that and we may need to prioritize, or add a final box, perhaps called Later Projects. Then we demolish the skyscraper by throwing every item into one of the boxes (or into the wastepaper bin if not assignable elsewhere).

This is Stage One, and is rather enjoyable. Stage Two drills us down a little further, so we should perhaps restrict it to our current concerns: Project A and Project C perhaps. We need some buff folders (or dynamic good-looking ones if we prefer), and we need to go through the Project A pile dividing the papers into:

- Actions – Now,
- Actions – Next,
- Reference material (including past events),
- Key documents.

That's it. Please don't buy a filing cabinet – at least not a big and remote one that sits, usually locked, in the corner. These four files should sit on your desk: sure, in a lovely looking file-holder if you fancy it. Big filing cabinets are for complete projects or maybe later projects, or even Project B. Meanwhile, anything that needs action *now* should be on the desk in front of you.

A note on electronic files: print them out. Apologies to environmentalists, but the paperless office is a myth. We need physical pieces of paper at this stage, so we should sweep through every electronic folder we have, and print out anything that shouldn't be immediately trashed (although perhaps putting those unallocated but want-to-save-anyway documents in a new electronic folder called 'want to save'). This is a cleansing process so we need to cleanse – thoroughly.

Of course, there are those that'll call me a Luddite for insisting on physical bits of paper – potentially making our organizational problems worse (or at least more cluttered). I'd ask them to locate one electronic file – just one – they had ten years ago. If, by some miracle, it's not only locatable but can still be opened and updated on a current computer, we also need to ask if it's still relevant. Come on, be honest – it's sat there doing nothing for all these years: lost, forgotten, unloved. Either use it or put it out of its misery. And, if you want to use it: print it, file it and put the file somewhere prominent.

## *Point Six*: Finish that plan

This is where we edit all that brainstorming. So far, we may have a jumble of disconnected thoughts and ideas: objectives and milestones, strategies and tactics, forecasts and schedules – all mixed up with process and procedure. And it may be scribbled on a list, scattered across a mind map or written as a 'stream of consciousness' document. However it's written, now we need to make sense of it all by creating a usable execution document.

These documents always look formidable – the result of bigger and more organized brains than our own. Yet look closely and they're remarkably similar to the filing exercise we've just completed.

All we do is put the – perhaps disparate – thoughts and ideas under a series of headings that make sense from a project-management perspective.

Harold Kerzner is perhaps the leading writer on project management, which he defines as 'the planning, organizing, and controlling of company [or individual] resources for a relatively short-term objective that has been established to complete specific goals and objectives'.

In his definitive 2006 guide *Project Management*, Kerzner states that many executives lose their jobs because they fail to manage the 'project management process'. In fact, process is the right word because execution is just that: a process. There's no special talent or attribute involved. We just need to write a plan, activate it, and keep going.

For Kerzner, planning involves 'selecting the enterprise objectives and establishing the policies, procedures, and programs necessary for achieving them'.

This sounds complex but, again, it's just the organization of random thoughts under headings.

These include:

- *Objectives* – what we aim to accomplish from the project. This is not our long-term goal but a project or milestone within.
- *Programme* – our action points for ensuring we meet our objectives.
- *Schedule* – any timing constraints or external deadlines, or simply our preferred timeframe for conception.
- *Budget* – anticipated costs (be realistic: underestimating the costs is a quick way to wreck your motivation).
- *Forecast* – our expected progress at certain points (i.e. what should be done when?).
- *Organization* – the resources required (human or otherwise).
- *Procedure* – those action points put into some form of sequential order.
- *Standards* – what are our benchmarks for success?

Of course, all this may look daunting. But it isn't. It's just filing for our thoughts.

## *Point Seven*: Write a checklist

The above looks like a lot of planning, but we're not done yet because we need a list. Lists are crucial because they turn our plans – which may be several thousand words long – into a series of one-or-two-word instructions, the most important of which is a checklist. Checklists differ from to-do lists in that they capture everything that has to be included to execute any element of our plan, while to-do lists capture everything to be done over a particular timeframe, including non-project related concerns.

If we go back to David Allen's example of moving offices then a checklist will include each element – agree location, source office, plan move, inform suppliers – while a to-do list may also include taking the dog to the vet and buying a birthday card for grandma. Of course, each line on our checklist could generate a supplementary list. 'Agree location' for instance could include: ask staff, ask clients, ask partner, quiz agents, check prices, check availability, check transport links.

Checklists contain a fantastic egalitarianism. They're simply a line on a list – there's no hierarchy. Of course, there can be many checklists – across all the aspects of our lives. Yet there should probably be only one to-do list or we're likely to confuse ourselves and forget something crucial.

Checklists are important. They're often the 'kick off' point for our actions – similar to pilots calling 'check' as they run down their pre-flight cockpit routine. With the 'checks' complete they're off down the runway, as are we once a particular checklist is complete. Yet checklists also work as the end-of-session or pre-break jotting of requirements for picking up where we left off (what Allen calls his 'memos to self').

## *Point Eight*: SWOT that strategy

So far, we've ignored strategy – largely because strategists spend too much time pondering, which can become a disabling trait for the productively challenged (who need no excuse to overthink things). Yet strategy is important because it's the key element for making sure our actions are focused on our objectives. Indeed, action without a strategy may well be wasted endeavour, no matter how well-honed those objectives.

Strategies, therefore, remove the headless-chicken approach to action – making sure that, as a chicken, we're heading in the right direction (while keeping our head). That said, a short passage on strategy in a book this broad cannot do justice to the enormous strategy industry – offering advice galore on how to go about developing and executing winning strategies.

So how about a shortcut? If strategies are focused on ensuring our actions are well targeted – and keep us moving towards our goal; and if we've developed a sequential series of steps towards our goal, then being strategic may simply be a case of knowing our strengths, and acting upon them. Of course, it also means knowing our weaknesses, as well as acting to overcome them.

To me, this sounds like a good excuse for a SWOT – a favourite tool of strategists because, as they all say, we need to ensure we have the right resources for the task in hand and are aware of the dangers. When assessing our plans, therefore, we should look at ourselves from an execution perspective, and list our current *strengths* and *weaknesses*, as well as the *opportunities* and *threats* we can see ahead.

Such an exercise should quickly tell us where immediate action is possible (our strengths), as well as where we may need to acquire new skills (our weaknesses). And it should point us to some short- and mid-term milestones (the opportunities), as well as some areas where we need to navigate (the threats).

Certainly, a SWOT gets us thinking strategically. Meanwhile, it's structured enough – and brief enough – to prevent us seeing it as an imposition or a hindrance.

## *Point Nine*: Focus

'The Law of Concentration states that whatever you *dwell* upon, grows', writes Brian Tracy in *Maximum Achievement* (1993). 'The more you think about something, the more it becomes part of your reality.'

For Tracy, this law explains both success and failure. Those that get things done are those that have developed the ability to concentrate on that *thing* – single-mindedly staying with it until completion.

Listen to any successful person – in business, sport or the arts – and they all talk about focus. It's an iron law of achievement.

'Effective people guard the doorways of their minds diligently', he continues. 'They remain focused on what's really important to them.'

Being linear is a key part of this. Our bulging plans and long checklists could overwhelm us without focus, which is why all the planning has to come down to some executable action points that are arranged in a linear (i.e. sequential) order, with each action-point benefiting from fierce concentration.

One last thing on focus: it's effective due to the way our brain is programmed. Our reticular activating system (RAS) is a set of connected nuclei in the brain stem that regulates the brain's arousal. In other words, the RAS is the filter through which our perception of the outside world travels – alerting us to what's important, ignoring what isn't.

The RAS is fantastically receptive to the information we need to find. Perhaps thanks to our hunter-gatherer past, it alerts us to both the threats and opportunities that our senses detect. Of course, everyone's RAS is different, meaning we are alerted to different things. For instance, my father was a structural engineer focused on building failure, which meant he was incapable of walking into a building without being alerted to its tiny flaws. Meanwhile, my eldest son likes football and can spot an Arsenal or Chelsea badge (perhaps in a shop window) from 50 metres.

For both my father and son, it's their RAS doing the work – filtering out the irrelevant, pointing out the relevant. Florists spot flowers, opticians spectacles, sub-editors newspaper typos. They're never off duty.

## *Point 10*: Make that call

Making plans that we fail to undertake is probably the most common act of self-sabotage for those seeking positive productivity. So if we hesitate here we're in 'good' (or at least common) company. Yet every word thus far written in this book is to get us to this point: the moment we act. Not to do so – to get to the brink and pull back – isn't just self-sabotage, it's self-betrayal.

Forget our conditions, forget our types, forget our past: from this moment onwards, we're one of two sorts of people. We're either someone that acts, or we're someone that fails to act. Having calculated our desires and long-term goals, therefore. And having drafted a plan, as well as having turned that plan into a checklist with its sequential action points: if we still hesitate we've as good as surrendered. Worse, we're fodder for those capable of action.

> **Get Things Done:** *You need to invest time and money creating a workstation you enjoy using, and then you need to use it: capturing everything, ordering it, completing your action plan and checklist and – mostly importantly – getting started.*

# 8

# MANAGING TIME

'Time is the only resource that must be spent the instant it is received', writes Alec Mackenzie in *The Time Trap*, the 1972 book that still outsells all others on the subject, 'and it must be spent at one fixed rate: sixty seconds per minute, sixty minutes per hour.'

Mackenzie's brilliance was in writing a treatise to time: a eulogy to the ticking clock. He taught us to value time – as in the quote above – and to respect it, as in the quote below.

'We cannot manage time,' he says. 'We can only manage ourselves in relation to time. We cannot control how much time we have; we can only control how we use it.'

Of course, he's tough on time wasting. But he accepts that time management contradicts the laws of human nature, so he's not surprised we allow innate human characteristics – such as our ego, our desire to please, our fear of offending, or our fear of the new – to override our inner concerns regarding the passing of unproductive time. Curiosity, insecurity, pride, envy, ambition, perfectionism – all are traits that can interfere with our time efficiency, says Mackenzie.

Yet he's also clear about where the fault lies.

'The true cause underlying most time wasters is found within the person who allows his or her time to be wasted', he concludes.

There's no getting away from it – it's up to us to maximize the utility of time. No one else will do it for us. We must examine ourselves, and be willing to change.

Mackenzie is adamant:

> 'To make progress with time management, you have to look squarely at your own habits and be willing to do the work of changing them.'

## Our ideal day

As ever, planning is the key. We need to set long-range goals and then plan backwards towards our current reality – filling in the gap with sequential and productive pursuits (as previously described). Yet Mackenzie implores us to add our own chemistry into the mix. We must understand our 'personal energy cycle' and use that as our guide for creating the 'ideal day', which means planning blocks of time moulded to our working preferences.

My day, for instance, begins with writing – because that's when I'm at my sharpest and most creative. By mid-morning, however, I'm written out but still with energy to plan and discuss objectives and strategies with my team or with clients, usually over coffee. By lunch I'm at my social peak and seek company: a client, a journalist, a team member or some other industry contact (obviously this takes some planning). By early afternoon, however, I'm ready to let other people do the thinking and talking, so this is a good time to schedule meetings with new or potential employees, or maybe a less taxing client meeting.

Yet the clock ticks on and, by 4 p.m., the urgency of the day is tugging at my conscience – making its remainder a strong period for administrative work, including scheduling future meetings and lunches. But I'm not finished yet. With no social engagement, I'd arrive home and spend some time with my children before their bedtime, my supper and a relaxing late evening spent reading around the subjects for tomorrow's writing session.

Of course, I can read the above and immediately dismiss it with an '*I wish*' – perhaps two days in the past month have kept to this pattern. Yet that's the point. This is the day we wish to have – a benchmark by which to measure every day, as well as the path we return to no matter how many times we're blown off course. We should expect and cope with interruptions (see below) – they're inevitable. But they shouldn't be the norm. Our *ideal day* – or as close as we can get to it – is the norm, and we should plan to make that norm a reality.

'Planning your day, rather than allowing it to unfold at the whim of others, is the single most important piece in the time-management puzzle', concludes Mackenzie.

## Dealing with interruptions

With respect to interruptions, Mackenzie is firm. He talks of controlling 'the whim of others', which is easily stated but far from easy to execute. The needs of others can crowd in on us like bullies in a playground. Yet, even here, Mackenzie is aware of the problems and offers some helpful tips (with added thoughts from elsewhere).

*1. Telephone interruptions*

It's a reflexive instinct to answer the phone, but that makes the phone our tormentor rather than our tool. All modern phones can take messages – so why don't we let it ring to voicemail and pick up the message during a break? It may even be worth switching mobile phones off (or putting them on silent) in the periods we're trying to concentrate, as long as we diligently return (relevant) calls at our designated time.

Of course, email is the new terror-tactic of the interrupter, yet – no matter what flags or exclamation marks are added to the note – we're the person in charge of when we read it, and when we respond. We just need to remind ourselves that these are *our* tools to make *us* more effective. They're not the instruments of torture others use to administer pain (more on proactive phone and email effectiveness in Part Three).

*2. Drop-in visitors*

Ineffective past behaviour may mean we've created a culture of expectation regarding casual visits from colleagues, friends and neighbours (this is equally true in the office or home). We welcome distraction, so encourage interruptions.

Yet that was our past. Spending mornings in delightful but irrelevant chatter may be fun, but it's the enemy of productivity. And while it may be awkward to disengage from other time-wasters, who we may have recruited or who may have sourced us as a fellow laggard, now is the time to change that culture. Without being rude, we can perhaps explain our new life-changing project and set out some boundaries with respect to the time-blocks required for execution.

Sorry, but if you're determined to change your behaviour in order to become more productive, clinging on to unproductive habits and people will simply drag you back. This may not be apparent in the short term, when willpower can overcome the temptations. But, over the long term – once the willpower has dissipated – it will.

There's no going back. And you may need to burn some bridges to prove this.

*3. Meetings*

'A meeting is an event where minutes are taken and hours wasted', said James T. Kirk, captain of the *Starship Enterprise*. In fact there are hundreds of such quotes – all stating that no other events in our working life are as disruptive to workflow as meetings.

Yet they can also produce strong results, says Mackenzie, as long as there's an agenda, they start on time and they've been pre-screened for their necessity (including of your attendance).

In my opinion, being trapped as a non-participant in an irrelevant meeting is one of the most frustrating workplace experiences possible. But being on top of the agenda, and being able to recruit attendees to *your* objectives, is among the most enabling: you just need to strategize for that result (more on productive and unproductive meetings in Part Three).

*4. Travel*

After meetings, travel is perhaps the greatest work-related interruption to workflow. Yet it shouldn't be. Sure, we must cut down on unnecessary travel. But this contradicts sales advice telling us to 'always get on the plane or train' in order to close the deal. Indeed, that's the problem with business travel – much of it can only be judged as meaningful in hindsight.

So, instead, we should try to maximize the opportunities travel brings. Again, by blocking out noise as best we can, we can use the chunks of time on planes or trains to research or write something requiring that length of endeavour. Indeed, the change of scene can be an aid to creativity, or at least perspective. Often the phrase or thought I wanted – or the elusive solution to a sticky problem – comes to me more readily as I stare out of the train window. Even overnight trips can be beneficial, with evening meals alone offering the chance to read more deeply into something than was previously possible.

Two things to add to this. First, plan for the journey. Make sure you have the materials you need, because – once the wheels start rolling – there's no going back. Second, where possible, avoid driving. To me, nothing looks more wasteful than being stuck in traffic – flustered by geography and with a mind full of speed cameras and road-signs. I love being on the train as it parallels a motorway – gliding past at speed as I glance up, notice the backed-up traffic, and then get back to that vital pre-meeting preparation.

*5. A bottleneck boss or shifting subordinate*

Interruptions can also take the form of passive barriers to progress – i.e. something that doesn't happen that needs to. And this can cause problems originating from those both above and beneath us on the hierarchy.

'A bottleneck boss acts as a pinch-point in the workflow, causing work to back up', opines the Harvard Business Essentials book of *Time Management* (2005), adding balance by also stating 'subordinates are only too eager to shift their problems onto their boss's back'.

Dealing with either isn't easy. Yet clarity of structure and role is important. If, from the outset of a project, there are clear demarcation points at which senior input is required we at least have a legitimate basis to judge interruptions: has the subordinate (including us if we're looking for input from above) reached the limits of their/our autonomy, or are they/we being lazy or overly fearful?

I often say to my team, 'never bring me a problem without having thought about the solution', which they sometimes interpret as a negation of duty on my part: am I not the problem-solver? In some cases they're right. I'm throwing the problem back at them in order to reduce the interruption. Yet it's done me no harm – and helped them develop their decision-making skills and, ultimately, their confidence (especially when we go with their solutions despite my own prejudices suggesting a different route).

Bosses are, of course, a trickier species – especially as many think nothing of loading trivial or administrative tasks on top of major project work. This can be depressing, although insisting on prioritization can help ensure they think beyond their own needs, which may be so diverse and cumbersome they've lost sight of their core objectives.

*6. Socializing*

Cut out socializing! Dear me, I do sound like a grouch, don't I? Of course, that's not what I'm saying. Yet Mackenzie has it right when he implores us to 'reduce *excess* socializing', which – of course – begs the obvious question: what constitutes excess?

Mackenzie asks us to look for cues regarding the limits of social time, which – in my view – means not stepping beyond the point at which our socializing cuts into our productive time: either physically or, more likely, from the hangover our socializing can induce.

If that next drink means we'll feel awful tomorrow, then avoid it. If our friends are determined to drag us to one more bar, or take in a last party or nightclub, and we know it'll have a detrimental impact on our ability to stick to our schedule, then we need to develop the mental strength to resist. We're not rejecting them – no matter what they say or how personally they take it at the time.

If we're determined to reach our goals – really determined – we have to be willing to make some sacrifices. And if we can't even cut out the excess – the icing on the icing – then we should surrender now and perhaps return to this book when feeling more capable of resisting that (vodka-laced) marshmallow.

*7. Too many tasks*

Finally, there's overcommitment. If we try to do too much, the tasks start interrupting each other and we end up developing a gnat-like attention span. Certainly, this is a major problem for me. The pressures of home, business and now writing – all bring with them the potential for interruption, exacerbating ADD-style characteristics.

Of course, we should try to eliminate tasks that can be delegated or are frivolous. But this may still mean more tasks than we can immediately handle. And this is where strong time-management – the parcelling up of time to deal with our various roles and responsibilities – can be useful. Stephen Covey (1989) uses a school-style timetable that divides up our every waking hour: from eight-til-eight, seven-days a week. Importantly, it includes a column for weekly goals against our different roles (in my case business owner, manager, writer, husband, father, son) and a daily list of priorities (that can also be our to-do lists).

'The key is not to prioritize what's on your schedule', says Covey, 'but to schedule your priorities.'

## Activity quadrants

Covey states that task overload is a result of our inability to prioritize. His thesis is that we spend too much time doing the wrong things, and to prove it he divides our every activity into one of four quadrants in his 'Time Management Matrix'.

Quadrant I: *Urgent and important.*
Quadrant II: *Not urgent but important.*
Quadrant III: *Urgent but not important.*
Quadrant IV: *Not urgent and not important.*

Inevitably, we spend most of our lives in the two quadrants marked 'urgent'. And while one involves important work (such as deadline-driven projects) the other (QIII – *urgent and not important*) is usually the realm of other people's interruptions. Meanwhile, we ignore Quadrant II, which is likely to be the work – such as research or relationship-building – that makes the most headway towards our long-term goals. In fact, despite its importance, Quadrant II is the least loved of all the quadrants because urgent work, once done, is often replaced by the trivial time-wasting of Quadrant IV (*not urgent and not important*) activities.

Of course, one reaction to this may be: 'tell me something I don't know'. Yet it's still a worthy exercise. If we know that too much time is spent in the unimportant Quadrants III and IV, for instance – or that we're trapped by urgent work that prevents us doing important work that's not urgent – we may be able to do something about it (such as using Covey's timetable to schedule Quadrant II work that still fits in with our personal energy cycle).

## To time log, or not?

That said, Covey's timetable poses a major dilemma for the time-challenged. While effective, it can sound like the sort of oppressive regime many of us have previously rebelled against. We must remember that unproductive people are adept at self-sabotage, so any regime that seeks to regiment our time may result in us falling off the wagon and ending up back at our ineffective worst.

Mackenzie only adds to the concern.

'To change a habitual pattern takes more conviction than you can build on sheer memory', he says. 'There's simply no better way than logging [your time] to get an accurate picture.'

We *have* to do this, he seems to state, which immediately feels like both an admonishment and an imposition.

Yet Covey's and Mackenzie's time structures are there to build awareness of the wasteful way this precious resource is currently squandered. And it's this awareness that's important – not the structure we choose as a potential solution.

Covey, Mackenzie, the Harvard Business School and others will, of course, implore us to adopt and retain *their* techniques. But they're organized people preaching to the disorganized, which is unfair. This is *their* world – so they adore time logs and timetables. And our struggles in this respect make their insistence that we create and stick to a timetable or time-log immediately off-putting.

In our hearts, we know we're never going to sustain such an involved endeavour.

## Instead, keep a diary

Nonetheless, we do need a self-correcting document that keeps us on track with respect to our use of time. And we also need a diagnostic tool for when we err – helping us learn the lesson and get back on the correct path as soon as possible. So why can't this be our diary – perhaps the A5 page-per-day diary mentioned earlier in Chapter 4?

With the lessons learnt (maybe via a two-week use of Covey's timetable) we can convert them into the narrative of our diary – including our daily priorities and weekly goals against our various (and potentially competing) roles. The diary is there to chart our course – day-to-day – not in any strict format that feels like a pair of handcuffs, but in a way that builds the chronicle of our lives.

We're on a journey that has to be planned and recorded. And by making use of a single document, especially something as user-friendly as a day-per-page diary, we're time-tracking in a way that suits our 'personal energy cycle'. Our daily planning – or to-do lists – can be listed at the top of each page, with our experiences in realizing those needs recorded in the space below.

It's one book, one document – handy, mobile and fun (or at least cathartic) to update. It corrals the chaos and orders it by the simple expediency of being on a single daily page.

I'm now on my tenth year of intense diary keeping, and I can honestly claim it's by far the strongest organizational habit I've ever adopted – my time wouldn't be anywhere near as productive without it.

**Get Things Done:** *Time is your most precious resource, as well as the one most easily lost. You need to create your 'ideal day' as a benchmark, and then develop strategies for dealing with interruptions. While timetables or time-logs may help (especially at first), the use of a page-per-day diary should be sufficient to allow you to plan and review your progress.*

# 9

# DEVELOPING GOOD HABITS

The last of Napoleon Hill's distilled needs for riches (or other attainment) – after desire, faith and plans – is persistence. We need to keep going despite the near-certainty we'll encounter set-backs and frustrations.

That said, Hill quickly loops persistence back to his primary need.

'The ease with which lack of persistence may be conquered will depend *entirely* upon the intensity of one's desire', writes Hill. 'Weak desires bring weak results, just as a small amount of fire makes a small amount of heat. If you find yourself lacking in persistence, this weakness may be remedied by building a stronger fire under your desires.'

Yet there's more to persistence than desire in my opinion. There's also routine. If we can turn something into a routine it becomes automatic – just a part of our daily existence like a morning shower or coffee. Indeed, routine is stronger than just about any other impulse (including desire) because it's reinforced, rather than undermined, by inertia. Routine is our default position – what we do when not distracted or diverted elsewhere. And that makes it vital for developing persistence.

Since becoming a parent I've realized the importance of routine. Without routine, both parent and child become disoriented, with nearly all the tantrums (from both) coming about due to routine's disruption. And, as adults, we use routine as the basis for going about our daily lives, and become grumpy if they're disturbed. We like to get the same train, sit at the same desk, do reasonably similar things during the day – and then head home around the same time: only to repeat the process (hopefully) tomorrow. Of course, it's nice to voluntarily break out of the routine – perhaps with a holiday. But we're comforted by the knowledge our routine awaits: the train still leaves, the chair sits vacant, our job remains open.

Involuntarily losing our routine can be a shock. Of course, this is true with major props, such as our job or home life. But it's also true when it comes to those mundane daily rituals. Disruptions discomfort us. Like stones thrown into a millpond – the ripples have to dissipate (into a new routine) before we can, once again, feel comfortable.

## Wasteful routines

So our love of routine can offer clues regarding our struggles to overcome our unproductive state. Perhaps we've fallen into an ineffective – or even wasteful – routine, with the inertia generated by all routines leading us, in this case, down a path to nowhere.

This is a common occurrence, wonderfully illustrated in the 2002 comedy *About a Boy*. Wastrel Will Freeman (Hugh Grant) declares himself amazed how his days are filled with apparently-important but utterly-pointless routines. He even deploys a seemingly-efficient organization for his indolent lifestyle – dividing his daily activities into 30-minute units consisting of elements such as having a bath (one unit), watching a quiz show (one unit), playing snooker (three units) etc.

'I often wonder if I'd even have time for a job,' he declares. 'How *do* people cram them in?'

So poor routines can develop almost unconsciously, and quickly grow to dominate our lives – making routine potentially a major prop for inefficiency.

Of course, the answer is to replace our weak routines with a stronger version. How we achieve this is the obvious next question, although – again – Napoleon Hill has the answer: habit. *Think and Grow Rich* repeatedly emphasizes the fact we're beholden to our habits, whether good or bad. Yet our habits are a choice within our control, claims Hill, which means good habits can and will result from sheer determination.

## The habit loop

Thankfully, today's writers are less proselytizing. In *The Power of Habit* (2012), *New York Times* journalist Charles Duhigg focuses on the extraordinary role habit plays with respect to even our simplest choices. He claims that neurological experiments in the 1990s found that habits are formed in the *basal ganglia*, a core area of the brain found even in animals such as fish or birds (that are not known for their intelligence). This means there's something deeply basic about habits. They're as automatic as breathing or swallowing in terms of brain function.

The habit-forming routine within our brain is part of a three-step loop, writes Duhigg. First, there's a trigger or *cue* telling our brain to go into automatic mode. This could be a sight, sound or smell – anything that creates a cue for unconscious action. Second, is the action itself – the *routine*. And third is the *reward*. The reward is key because that's why the cue has triggered the routine: to get the reward.

Of course, it's easy to see how bad habits such as smoking or alcohol addiction develop from the cue–routine–reward loop. Yet good habits such as using toothpaste also emerge from the same loop. Indeed, as Duhigg points out, this more positive habit (of brushing our teeth) offers clues regarding how to build persistence from developing good habits.

He uses the example of *Pepsodent* – a toothpaste popularized by Claude Hopkins, an advertising pioneer working in the US around 1900. His early advertising for the product focused on 'tooth film', as he called *mucin plaques* (a naturally occurring membrane that had previously gone largely unnoticed). In fact, Pepsodent was no more effective at ridding teeth of the film than eating an apple, but that didn't stop Hopkins running campaign ads telling people to run their tongue across their teeth in order to feel the film (the cue). Once felt, the only way to remove the film, claimed the ads, was through using Pepsodent (the routine), which left teeth feeling and looking clean (the reward).

Sales of Pepsodent soared. Soon it was selling worldwide and led to a leap in American toothpaste use from 7 percent of households prior to Pepsodent to 65 percent just ten years' later.

And, according to Duhigg, the same formula can develop habits right across the behavioural spectrum.

'Studies of people who have successfully started new exercise routines, for instance,' says Duhigg, 'show they are more likely to stick with a workout plan if they choose a specific cue, such as running as soon as they get home from work, and a clear reward, such as a beer or an evening of guilt-free television.'

'It explains everything,' concludes Duhigg, 'from why it's so hard to ignore a box of doughnuts to how a morning jog can become a nearly effortless routine.'

Duhigg quotes a 2002 study by the New Mexico State University that sets out to understand the power of cravings in creating habits. It examined 266 individuals with a workout habit of at least three times a week. While many had taken up exercise on a whim – perhaps because they had spare time or were stressed – the reason they continued (to the point it became an ingrained habit) was due to the specific reward the exercise triggered. It made them 'feel good' was the answer of 92 percent of respondents in one group, meaning they craved the endorphins and other neurochemicals that exercise released.

So, while the cue could be simple – such as leaving your running shoes by the bed so they're their first sight each morning – the reward is specific, with one (the cue) immediately triggering the routine that would deliver the other (the reward).

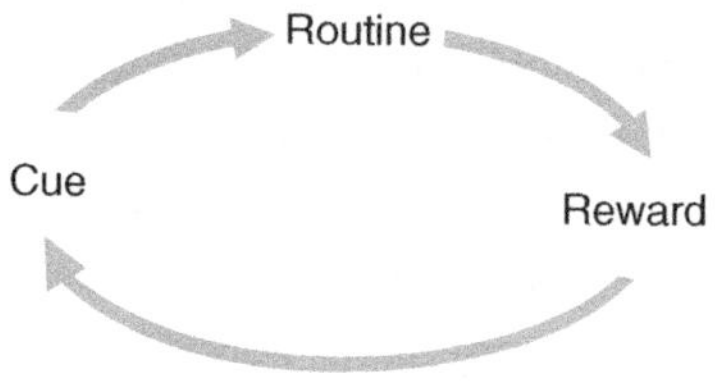


**Figure 3** Charles Duhigg's cue–routine–reward loop

## Bad habit replacement

Duhigg's book is wonderfully liberating for the unproductive person. It simply says we've developed disabling cue–routine–reward habits. Yet, once recognized as such, they can be replaced with more enabling ones. Perhaps boredom (the cue) triggers the routine of surfing the internet or leaving our desk that delivers the reward (stimulation). Perhaps distraction (the cue) triggers the routine of going to the vending machine that delivers the reward (chocolate-induced serotonin release). Or maybe anxiety (the cue) triggers the routine of distraction that delivers the reward (avoiding tackling our problems).

However we organize it, habits may be the reason we remain unproductive, despite our full knowledge they're potentially damaging our long-term prospects.

Certainly, I recognized my own behaviour within Duhigg's descriptions, but then I also realize I've done something about my bad habits that fits well with Duhigg's suggestions regarding making habits work for us rather than against us. For instance, five years ago I gave up drinking alcohol. No, I didn't have a drink problem (at least by UK middle-class standards). But I'd become concerned by the potentially corrosive impact on my brain of my habitual intake (my father had been diagnosed with Alzheimer's in this period).

So I decided to give up alcohol – switching from an alcohol habit to a coffee habit after reading that caffeine helps ward off Alzheimer's. Of course, I can report that my caffeine addiction's progressing nicely – triggered by various cues (smelling coffee, seeing others with a coffee, passing a favoured coffee chain) that trip me into the routine of buying (or making) coffee and the reward of enjoying the taste and feeling stimulated. I'd replaced a bad habit with a better (but not perfect) one – good for me.

Yet Duhigg would also be impressed by other positives centred around my caffeine habit. Writing books and running a company isn't easy. So I get to work at 6.45 a.m. in order to write until 9.30 a.m. Yet coffee is an important part of this routine. I couldn't start without it or even get out of bed without knowing that a coffee is the reward. That said, by mid-morning it's no longer caffeine I crave but exercise. I'm cued to go to the gym and use that routine to generate my 'feel good' reward.

In fact I use habits to get me through the day: coffee to get me started at 6.45 a.m.; another coffee to switch me over to company matters at 9.30 a.m.; exercise to deal with my mid-morning flag; lunch and a cup of tea to lever me towards an afternoon's productivity; and a sweet reward (naughty I know) to squeeze that last hour before my cycle home, which releases further endorphins for an hour or so playing with the kids.

While not all these habits are good, they're all geared towards one thing: productivity. I've replaced my unproductive habits (distraction, alcohol, anxiety) with productive ones (coffee, exercise, work) that bring me new rewards (endorphins, stimulation, progress towards my goals) – a resolution that groups such as Alcoholics Anonymous (AA) would fully endorse.

'In order to offer alcoholics the same rewards they get at the bar,' says Duhigg, 'AA has built a system of meetings and companionship – the "sponsor" each member works with – that strives to offer as much catharsis as a Friday night bender. If someone needs relief, they can get it from talking to their sponsor or attending a group gathering, rather than toasting a drinking buddy.'

The aim is to keep the cue, and retain the reward, while inserting a new routine in the middle. And, if we apply this to our own unproductive habits, we can – with thought and effort – convert them into more productive ones that help reinforce Hill's need for persistence.

## Self-addiction and its consequences

Bad habits may not be so easily eradicated, however – especially if we can't even recognize them for what they are. According to Noah Blumenthal, business coach and author of *You're Addicted to You* (2007) any repetitive action that doesn't enhance your life, but that you cannot stop doing – such as getting up too late or talking too much or bitching about others – could be what Blumenthal calls 'self-addiction'. These are negative habits that disable us. They may be unconscious or, if conscious, we may dismiss them as part of our character. Yet we have developed these behavioural habits through our failure to tackle them, allowing them to become a self-addiction.

'Behaviours that outlive their original purpose do so because at some point they become self-reinforcing', says Blumenthal. 'Many behaviours that start out healthy turn unhealthy over time'.

Yet Blumenthal is convinced we *can* change. To do so, he says, we need to deal with the problem in three parts.

In *Part One* we must begin by learning to identity our self-addictions. We can do this by, first, contrasting our behaviour with those around us. What actions and reactions do we not like about ourselves but cannot seem to stop? Negativity is one of my own, for instance – always looking for the downside and, inevitably, finding it.

Then we should allow this to shock us. As with my friend snapping and exploding a few of my self-built myths regarding my unhappy state and its causes – we should imagine being told off by a friend or associate who's finally had enough of our poor behaviour. Secretly, we knew it was coming: so let's do it to ourselves before they do it to us.

Blumenthal's *Part One* ends with a commitment to change. Having written down your self-addictions – using your diary – you should write down specific goals. But you also need to understand your motives for change. For instance, if I want to tackle my addiction to negativity, I should focus on my key motive for changing, which is the fact my negativity portrays me in a poor light with others. My goal of developing positivity, therefore, is aligned with my desire to radiate a more positive attitude publicly.

## Building support

*Part Two* involves 'building support'. In fact, this is as much about losing support as building it because we may have to identity the people that encourage our addictions or unhealthy behaviours and – literally – move away from them. These are the 'co-conspirators' – the 'partners in crime' we enrol as our allies when indulging our poor behaviour. Once our friends – legitimizing our behaviour – they're now the very people chaining us to the seabed of our self-addiction.

Yet 'co-conspirators' are not our only barriers in terms of people, according to Blumenthal. There's the 'pessimist' who thinks we cannot change, the 'admirer' who thinks we're great as we are (and may fear the changes taking place), and the 'avoider' who simply pretends there's nothing wrong.

Unfortunately, once identified, Blumenthal's pretty adamant: these relationships have got to go, to be replaced by supporters, who come in three main flavours.

- 'Knowing partners' – who you tell about the positive changes you're trying to make,
- 'Informing partners' – who offer feedback and monitor your progress,

- 'Working partners' – who are your new partners for change, working with you to help make the positive change.

As you may have spotted, this all sounds like the sponsors used by AA to keep the newly sober on track, which is exactly Blumenthal's ploy: to develop a 'circle of support' that helps reinforce the changes being made and to celebrate the successes.

Of course, we must also remember that many of our self-addictions are far from extreme. My negativity, for instance, is disabling but hardly life-threatening: I just tend to see threats more clearly than I see opportunities. If I've recruited a few pessimistic allies along the way, it seems a tad unfair to dump them – a move that may result in dramas I could do without. Far better to make them 'knowing partners' – telling them about my need for change and trying to enlist their support, while also looking to widen my network to include those that can aid my new outlook.

Finally, in *Part Three*, we have to take action. What does our new behaviour look and feel like in reality, and how do we reach that healthier spot? This may involve modelling our actions on others who've succeeded at our desired behaviour, and it should include keeping a record of our actions (in the usual place).

**Get Things Done:** *Persistence is as much a function of routine as determination, and routine is supported by your habits. Bad habits can impede productivity but can be replaced by good habits through understanding how habits develop. Self-addictions, meanwhile, can encompass all negative behaviours and require strong support to eradicate.*

# 10

# MAKING DECISIONS

Our final tool to help us get things done focuses on decision-making, not least because so many people are appalling decision-makers. Certainly, I was a terrible decision-maker and still have my battles in this respect, usually because I struggle to remove the emotions from my evaluations. Too often, I'm so concerned about my fragile self-esteem I cannot make cool judgements based on my long-term objectives.

No less disabling, I can almost instantly regret any decision. If the positives from any choice loomed large prior to the decisions; once made, it's purely the negatives that come into view. And this can lead to regret and what I call 'mental paralleling' in which I fantasize about the perfect and glorious alternative existence I could be enjoying if only I'd made the other choice.

## Decisions made at four levels

Mental paralleling is wasteful and exhausting, although I'm right about one thing: good decision-making is an absolutely vital requirement, and one we must understand on our journey towards strong productivity.

In *Wharton on Making Decisions* (2001) – a series of articles by professors of that famed business school, presented by Stephen J. Hoch and Howard C. Kunreuther – the claim is that decisions are made at four levels: individual (often emotionally driven); as a manager of others (often more formulaic); in negotiation (based on either co-operative or conflictual interactions); and societal (which may be based on principles or values).

Of course, this suggests our primary decision-making level – the personal – is the most emotional and therefore least logical. One of the articles – by Mary Frances Luce, John W. Payne and James Bettman (called 'The Emotional Nature of Decision Trade-Offs') – focuses on this conundrum, claiming that most people seek 'normative' (or 'ideal') judgements based on what they consider appropriate criteria, although this is usually corrupted by the desire to minimize negative emotions. And this may lead to decision-making based on avoiding difficult emotions, rather than seeking the ideal solution.

They offer the example of 'downsizing' a department, with the decisions on who to keep based, not on job skills or future needs, but on the family situations of those affected.

'As the stakes of a decision increase, the desire to find the best normative solution may coexist with the desire to manage or minimize one's negative emotions', they write.

Such concerns can lead to procrastination, with difficult decisions parked or kicked along the timeline as a form of avoidance. Yet if we can recognize upfront the influence our emotions play – and treat them as just one (though legitimate) factor in the decision – we can avoid them being so disabling, they claim. In the downsizing example this could include job skills, costs, other needs and – yes – the personal consequences for those involved. So emotions are given a legitimate but not dominant place in the process.

Adding to the difficulties here, however, is the issue of 'confirmation bias'. This means we give more weight to information that confirms our current views – including to emotions such as desire, dislike or fear – which may lead to decisions based purely on prejudice rather than reasoning.

Getting beyond confirmation bias is difficult, although Wharton suggests we focus on our long-term goals and use those as our benchmarks when trying to overcome the barrier of our own emotions or prejudices. In fact, by developing a strong bias towards our long-term objectives, we're recruiting the potential distortions of 'confirmation bias' to our needs.

## Risk, benefits and costs

Meanwhile, Wharton's business school rival Harvard takes a more pragmatic approach – as offered in *Decision Making*, the 2006 Harvard Business Essentials guide.

'In many respects a business [or individual's progress] is a series of decisions linked by implementation and other activities', it states, before adding that decisions are an inevitable trade-off between the potential 'risks, benefits and costs' of any decision.

So how do we make the trade-off? Like Wharton, they recommend that we extrapolate the decision in this case into all three components. Yet this will only help once we can successfully weight the importance of each – a personal concern that brings in Napoleon Hill's notions of desire and faith, as well as worries regarding fears and prejudices.

Weighting dilemmas aside (see below), Harvard asks us to follow a logical process when making decisions.

We must:

1. *Establish the context of the decision.* What, exactly, is being decided? This may not be obvious (especially if our emotions are in the way). Also, what's the key criteria for evaluating the decision (costs, speed, quality), as well as the critical factors that may dictate our preferences (money, time, security, or – hopefully – something that supports our long-term objectives)?
2. *Frame the issue.* As pollsters know, the answers we get are determined by the questions we ask, so it's important to avoid confirmation bias when deciding upon the actual decision required. A recent example is the Scottish independence referendum question, which originally began with the suggestive

supposition 'do you agree . . .' which was judged as inviting the answer 'yes'. So we must frame the question neutrally (or as neutrally as possible). Indeed, poorly formed questions may end up with us making decisions aimed at dealing with the wrong issue, or even an invented one that acts as a surrogate for the real concerns.

3. *Develop good alternatives*. Of course, we may (in fact, will probably) have a bias for a single alternative, and will spend time seeking confirmation that our 'gut instincts' are correct. Yet gut instincts are often based on poor conditioning which, as we have seen, can negatively distort perspectives. So we must develop a list of alternatives, even if this seems, at first, forced.
4. *Evaluate the alternatives*. Indeed, many of our invented alternatives may be pure baloney, so an evaluation is required. Which of these choices are feasible? What will they cost in terms of time, money or resource? Is that affordable? And is cost the key criteria for evaluation? If having trouble we can utilize Harvard's 'prioritization matrix', which lists the alternatives before scoring each (perhaps out of ten) on various indicators. These are then weighted for importance although, again, this raises concerns regarding weighting.
5. *Select the best alternatives*. This is the difficult bit, with even Harvard falling back on platitudes such as 'this step can be a challenge' or recommending we set a deadline for the decision. Again, a reference to our long-term goals should support our judgement.

## Decision trees

Using a 'decision tree' may help. This is similar to a mind map, although (usually) runs left to right. Unsurprisingly, decision trees look like trees, although ones lying on their side – making my preferred metaphor (perhaps due to my childhood fantasies) railway branch lines diverging away from a city-centre terminal.

Immediately out of the station will be the key choice or dilemma – a 'yes' or 'no' dichotomy perhaps (or more likely a comparison between two alternatives) – with further alternatives branching out as we head for the suburbs.

So, if our central dilemma is, say, 'shall we launch a new product?' the first two lines out may simply say 'yes' and 'no' with branch lines from 'yes' saying (perhaps if we're a clothes retailer) 'shirts' or 'skirts', with branch lines from 'no' perhaps saying 'reduce number of lines' or 'retain current number of lines' – and so on. The result should be a diagram that lines up a series of alternative outcomes that, while complex-looking, can be readily understood, even if we've yet to decide the basis for making a decision.

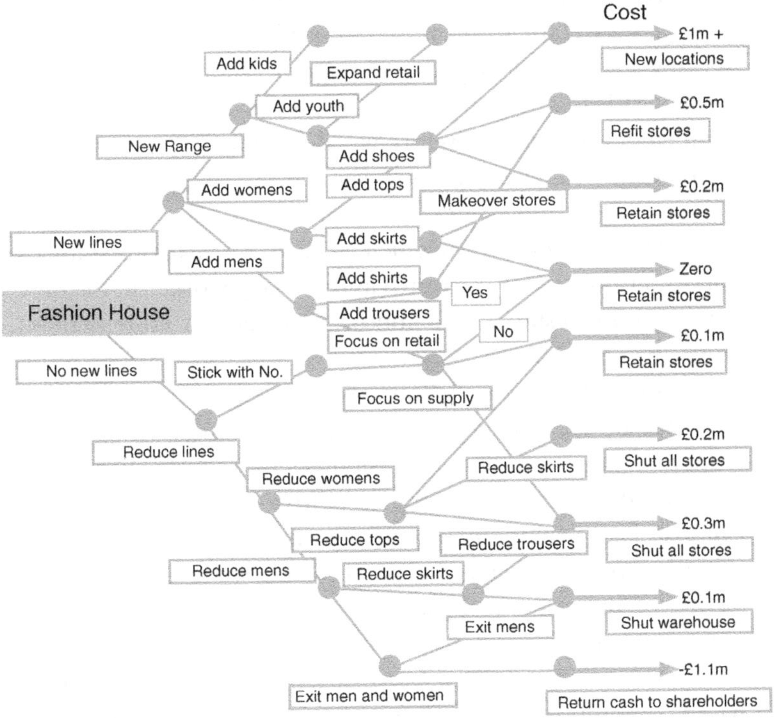


**Figure 4** A decision tree showing the options available to a fashion house

In fact, nearly all textbook examples result in a monetary list on the right-hand end of the diagram, or some other empirical (i.e. measurable) outcome. These figures are usually no more than guesses and may not even be the most useful criteria for making a decision, which takes us right back to 'establishing the context' of what we're trying to decide.

## Avoiding 'rule of thumb' thinking

Yet difficulties remain. The confirmation bias mentioned above is what's known as a 'heuristic' or 'rule of thumb'. Nearly everyone employs these when making decisions, often with disastrous consequences, says Harvard professor Max H. Bazerman.

Writing in *Judgement in Managerial Decision Making* (2005), Bazerman calls this 'System 1 thinking', which is intuitive, immediate and emotional, and therefore worth avoiding.

Other common heuristics include:

*The 'availability heuristic'*, in which we focus on factors that appear important because of their proximity. A lazy worker in the office next door, for instance, will annoy a manager far more than one down the corridor.

*The 'representative heuristic'*, in which a judgement is based on incorrect or incomplete generalizations. Prejudicial statements such as 'people from [this/that country] are lazy, so [X] will also be lazy' form part of the 'representative heuristic', although it can also lead to misconceptions regarding chance. For instance we may continue playing cards because we're on a 'winning streak' or because our 'luck *must* change' – assuming there's a pattern to entirely random probabilities.

And then there's the '*affect heuristic*', in which judgements are based on emotions or intuition, not on logic. The potential bias here is unlimited because we dismiss people or decisions based on entirely invented suppositions, such as our 'sixth sense'.

'There's something about him/her I don't like' or 'I have a funny feeling about this', which is usually fear of the unknown or even our prejudicial conditioning.

Certainly, heuristics are deeply ingrained decision-making habits that can lead to a lifetime of flawed decisions, states Bazerman. Yet they're not our only decision-making challenge. Another is the 'non-rational escalation of commitment', which may encourage us to continue investing in something that's not working out – say a failing subordinate – in the hope that the new investment will prevent the original investment from being wasted.

This is what's termed 'throwing good money after bad': something we may also do with other resources, such as time, effort or even love. Yet the previous investment, says Bazerman, was a 'sunk cost' and should therefore no longer figure in our decision-making.

## The weighting dilemma

Both Wharton and Harvard focus on organizations, or at least on teams, which means they quickly lose resonance for individuals – perhaps as we stare out of the kitchen window on the horns of a dilemma. Indeed, much of the analysis is aimed at eradicating 'groupthink' – the creation of potentially false consent due to the conscious or unconscious avoidance of team conflict. Certainly, one has only to think of the oppressive groupthink that led to Japan's decision to attack Pearl Harbour in 1941 to realize the potential consequences in this respect. Yet it's hardly our most pressing concern as an individual trying to make decisions while alone.

And, for individuals, it's often the 'weighting' dilemma that weighs most heavily upon us: how do we turn off our fears or other emotions in order to judge correctly the importance of one element in comparison with another?

The great man Mackenzie may have the answer. In *The Time Trap*, he spends many pages focused on turning our overarching goals into parcelled-up objectives that require prioritizing for execution. Such a logical process helps get us beyond the brink of a decision because it offers compelling criteria for both evaluation and action. Is this the required next step – a question that should help circumnavigate those potentially emotional concerns?

That said, Mackenzie offers further help by invoking Pareto's 80/20 law as a device for weighting the components of a decision. Vilfredo Pareto was a nineteenth century Italian thinker who demonstrated that, by 1893, 80 percent of Europe's wealth was in the hands of 20 percent of the population – a major improvement in social mobility, in fact, as prior to industrialization wealth was far more intensely concentrated. Yet Pareto's law is now most often associated with the assumption that 20 percent of our tasks or effort yield 80 percent of the results (which is how Mackenzie employs it).

To me, this is a fantastically enlightening concept, not least because it offers us a benchmark for the weighting of decision-making criteria. Given that most decisions are, in reality, a series of choices regarding the application of resources, we can now evaluate them by seeking the 20 percent of resource application likely to yield 80 percent of the desired result.

Of course, we need to factor in risk: the likelihood that we'll achieve such a result (it may require a lot more than 20 percent and achieve well below 80 percent). But even here we now have a strong benchmark: our guess at the probabilities of meeting Pareto's 80/20 rule.

In fact, entrepreneur Richard Koch was so taken by 80/20 thinking that he wrote a series of books imploring us to convert our entire lives into 80/20 judgements. Koch's claim is that this is a universal law: 'All human history, all progress in civilization, involves getting more with less,' he writes in *Living the 80/20 Way* (2005), adding that the law applies to all animals, groups and individuals.

Does the decision you make give you not only a better solution, but an easier one, he asks? Because unless it's both it's unlikely to lead to sustainable improvements.

Of course, life's not so simple. Other responsibilities crowd in on us constantly, although Pareto's law can help us decide between equal alternatives by calculating which one is the slow-and-reluctant donkey, and which one the seemingly effortless Porsche.

**Get Things Done:** *Emotions shouldn't be ignored in decision-making. They should just be one factor in an extrapolated process that tries to remove prejudices and other 'rules of thumb' while focusing on our long-term objectives. Pareto's 80/20 law can help decide between competing equals.*

# PART THREE

# Get Things Done . . .

# 11

# . . . ON THE PHONE

Sure it can feel a little dated, but one book I love reading – just for its sheer chutzpah – is *What They Don't Teach You at Harvard Business School* (1984) by sports management pioneer, Mark H. McCormack.

For McCormack, it's the practical stuff that matters. And for work-hours productivity, his view is simple: get phone calls and meetings under control, and everything else will fall into place; although, if writing today, McCormack would no doubt include email.

We deal with meetings and email in later chapters: in McCormack's 1970s and 1980s heyday, the phone was *the* office terrorist, and remains an irritant to be reckoned with, not least because it's now in our pocket. So how do we make the telephone our servant rather than our master?

McCormack's primary, if rather surprising, tip is to seldom accept calls. He wants time to think about a phone call rather than be flustered by the interruption of someone calling. Refusing the call – or these days simply letting it ring to voicemail – means he can decide whether, and – if so – when, to return the call. He can also calculate what the caller is likely to want, as well as his preferred response.

If unable to avoid the call he quickly tries to gather his thoughts – perhaps injecting a false delay (such as a made-up caller 'on the other line'): anything to give him some time mentally to prepare for the call.

I'd certainly agree with this. Some of the most regretful telephone conversations I've ever had – some still burning in my memory – came about from taking calls when unprepared. It's a no-brainer: we wouldn't expect to start a 100-metre sprint the second we wake up – especially with our opponent fully prepared. So we're bound to be at a major, and unnecessary, disadvantage when taking a call without warning.

Equally, when making a call, McCormack implores us always to plan what we want to say. If necessary, write a short script or some bullet points. We should also know what constitutes success for the call and have in mind our approach for achieving it.

'If you're not crystal clear in your own mind what you want to accomplish,' says McCormack, 'you probably won't end up accomplishing it.'

And quickly get to the point of a call, he adds. Most callers are keen to waste time at the start of a call, assuming there's need for a warm-up. But this leaves you not knowing whether the call is valuable or not. Far better, says McCormack, to attack the crux of the call head-on and then add some personal points at the end, but only once you've got what you need and know that the call's been productive.

Of course, this may require firmness. Sales callers, in particular, have a habit of going around the houses – perhaps trying to 'build rapport' with their 'prospect'. It quickly irritates me (and McCormack) and I always cut in with a curt 'what can I do for you?' which usually gets them to the point.

## Make calls work

McCormack takes call scheduling very seriously – producing a list of the calls he needs to make (with numbers) and estimating a time for each call, which he then tries to stick to. He even conjures an ending if necessary, perhaps through a manufactured meeting that's about to start or a visitor in reception. Certainly, he says, once you have what you need from a call you should try to end it as soon as possible (or at least change the subject).

I'd heartily agree with this. Many is the time I've achieved my call objective and then nearly blown it by continuing to sell my need – a classic insecurity of the under-confident. Yet, it's obvious that if you keep fighting after victory's declared there's only one other possible result: *defeat!*

That said, McCormack is keen we accomplish something from every call. If our goal (however small) isn't achieved, we should try to get a time/date for a definite response (even if just for a follow-up call). If that's not possible, get a date for them to consider a follow up. And, if that's not achievable, we should just forget it says McCormack.

'Any further pursuit is almost certainly going to be a waste of time, and just in knowing this you've already accomplished a great deal', he concludes.

McCormack also has a lot to say about phone tag – that wasteful game in which we're constantly leaving messages for each other. His view: don't play it. This can be achieved by not leaving a message for them to call back but, instead, stating a time *you* will call them, which keeps you in charge of the process.

If dealing with another human (perhaps a PA) it's worth trying to explore the right time to call back, although McCormack also suggests a cheekier approach: leaving a longer message with your stated intentions, and asking them to call back if they disagree. Of course, while fine for someone with McCormack's executive clout, for the rest of us this may lead to wasted endeavour as we pursue projects others haven't agreed, although it makes a reasonable bluff if we think the other party's stalling.

## Establishing red zones

*The Time Trap*'s Mackenzie also has a lot to say about what he calls the 'untamed telephone'. For instance, he insists that we establish red zones for priority or proactive work that brook no interruptions from the phone. These should be periods in our 'ideal day' that are focused on nothing other than productive and goal-oriented activity.

We can even reverse this and allow calls *only* at certain times (perhaps two one-hour periods twice a day) – even stating this on voicemail greetings or automatic email replies. That said, we need to be careful that our wording doesn't sound pompous or feel like a brush-off.

In fact, Mackenzie's keen we use our voicemail greeting dynamically. We should learn how to change both our landline and mobile greeting and then refresh it every day – stating that 'we're in the office today and taking calls but busy between nine and eleven' or 'we're out of the office but will pick up messages by four'. This gives a strong impression of being on top of our work but still keen to hear from the outside world – once we can fit them in.

But if we do this we *must* keep it up – out-of-date voicemail greetings give the opposite impression (so avoid giving a date, just in case). And it may seem a bit of a stretch after a while – so a singular greeting can be nearly as dynamic if done well. 'This is Jim. I'm unavailable right now. Please leave a name and number, and a detailed message and I'll try to get back to you as soon as I can'.

The added bonus here is that we've already begun the call-screening process – helping to filter out calls from strangers: perhaps cold-calling salespeople keen to waste our time (in order to increase their 'success-rate' or 'effective calls' ratio).

And then there's the quirky advice of UK personal development guru Michael Heppell, in his book *How to Save an Hour Every Day* (2011). His roving eye alights on the phone but briefly, although long enough to offer some salient tips, especially for mobiles (with some thoughts of my own).

- Always save the number – even if there's only the 'remotest chance you may ever want to speak to them again'.

- As well as pre-framing the call, preframe the ending: 'Well I'm happy we've covered everything, thanks for that,' is his preferred precursor to a 'goodbye'.
- Stand up when on the phone. Don't get comfortable.
- Yes, *do* leave a message (always), although this doesn't have to be a passive plea for a return call. As with McCormack's advice, we could state our intention to call back in one hour or tomorrow at 9 a.m.; or, again, we could simply state our intentions, and ask them to call back if that's a problem.

**Get Things Done:** *The telephone remains a key irritant, so turn it into a tool. Rarely accept incoming calls, be disciplined and proactive with outgoing calls, and use voicemail dynamically – perhaps trying to get things to the next stage.*

# 12

# . . . USING EMAIL

Email is the juggernaut of modern office communications – dominating process to the point that its awesome power cannot be ignored. At least that's the zeitgeist. In reality, its dominance means that its power is assumed when, in fact, as a communications tool its power is exaggerated. Oddly, email is a device for the meek – allowing them to hide behind their computer screen rather than pick up the phone or meet face-to-face. And this can make us overly brave – turning the coward into a suicide bomber, which makes email more a hazard to navigate than a power to harness.

Certainly, email's ability to persuade is weaker than the phone or a meeting and sometimes weaker than a well-targeted piece of snail mail. Yet it's not going away anytime soon, so email has to be dealt with, although (note from the advice below) that the main concern of the experts is limiting the potential damage caused by email.

At best, email has quickened the pace of the business process – allowing formal communication to proceed at a hasty clip when it was formerly at what now looks like a leisurely stroll. Entire purchases, complex negotiations or formal documentations can be completed in hours (if not minutes) when they would have taken days (if not weeks). But this doesn't make the medium revolutionary: just quick.

At its worst, email destroys communication, erodes relationships and kills nuance. It can also waste as much time as it saves. Uncontrolled email can take over – making it the enemy of productivity (a far cry from its intended role as an aid to communication).

## A fantastic tool if . . .

Julie Morgenstern has written a series of books aimed at both personal and workplace organization. With names like *Organizing From The Inside Out* (2000) and *Never Check Email in The Morning* (2005), her key aim has been to focus our attention on controlling workplace displacement behaviour, with an obvious and primary target being email.

She's asking us to realize that – when it comes to workplace inefficiency – the problem is usually us, not those harassing us (most often via email). Morgenstern considers modern innovations such as the Internet and email fantastic tools if properly managed. Not properly managed, and they become tyrannical beasts able to eat time and terrorize our process.

We must tame the beast, which brings us to her central email suggestion: to create a 'cone of electronic silence' by resisting looking at email for the first 60 minutes of our working day. To look is to risk our entire day being hijacked by reactivity when our aim should be to pursue proactivity (i.e. setting and pursuing our own agenda).

And, if this sounds unrealistic, think of its other key benefit for workplace efficiency: avoiding the regretted reply. This is one of my worst traits – firing off an emotionally charged email, usually in response to someone else's emotionally charged email, and then almost instantly wishing I hadn't. The day is as good as lost, as I fret, backpedal, fret some more, backpedal some more, seek reassurance from everyone around me, and ultimately give ground. All of which could have been avoided if I'd just controlled my email reaction time.

In fact, this is easily done by creating one morning pomodoro session to read emails and another – later – session for replying (perhaps leaving any particularly tricky ones overnight).

Even Mackenzie has something to say on this one – extending it to the 'chilly tone' of many emails.

'Ah, but we're so hooked on the easy technology,' he writes in a later edition of *The Time Trap*, 'we use it for everything. Only later, do we realize that we ought to have picked up the phone or visited the person we wanted to influence . . . The time we hoped to save by using email must now be spent repairing damaged feelings and rebuilding trust.'

## Avoiding email landmines

Certainly, email is more open to misinterpretation than any other medium (except texting – see below). There's something about the immediacy, the everyday language and the fact that written 'tone' is difficult to discern that means many emails are read in a different 'voice' from the one intended, causing unnecessary offence.

Yet avoiding such landmines is not difficult:

- *State your tone from the outset.* 'This is not an angry email', 'I write as a friend', 'please read this in the friendly tone in which it is written' – that sort of thing (although such notes can equally raise our guard, confirming that email really is a poor medium for anything emotional).
- *Say hi.* Always use the 'Hi [Jim/John/Jane],' greeting – it's simply become the norm for friendly emails.
- *Mind your language.* Avoid words such as 'wrong', 'mistake' and even 'you' in any negative context. 'I think/feel' is much better than 'you are' (because you're stating your feelings rather than projecting deniable accusations onto others). Words such as 'may' and 'could' also help remove the hardness or starkness

of any instruction or reprimand. And any form of accusatory or hierarchical language should be avoided. For example, writing 'you were wrong to do this,' will immediately generate a defensive response. If, instead, we write 'I feel something went wrong on this project: let's discuss,' we're stating our feelings (which they cannot deny) while avoiding being accusatory. And, rather than throwing hand grenades from behind a wall, we're inviting them to offer their view first,

- *Don't be an informal emailer.* To anyone other than close friends, you should send only professionally constructed and well-written emails. While this may seem counter-intuitive, it's the inconsistency in tone – the loss of informality as you address a serious subject – that most often unintentionally offends. I always ask employees to adopt the tone of a country solicitor, who may be friendly but is never overly familiar or lax in his/her choice of words,
- *If genuinely annoyed, avoid email.* It's a horrible medium for soothing differences, with users quickly entrenched and hurling abuse. Certainly, I've solved flaming email rows with colleagues after a few minute's face-to-face. It's a lesson worth learning – email (perhaps due to the anonymity of the keyboard and the ease of clicking 'send') puts us at our least conciliatory.

## Tackling the randomness of email

Having caught up with the technology, Mackenzie offers plenty of thoughts on what he calls the 'randomness of electronic interruptions'. These include (with added thoughts of my own):

- *Control inbox activity.* As with Morgenstern, Mackenzie is keen to put email in its place – even suggesting turning off the incoming signal (or not opening your email account) until an allotted time, just to remove the temptation. Of course, smartphones make this more difficult but, in each case, we must remember that these are *our* tools. We control them, so discipline yourself to deal with email twice or at most four times a day, he states – at the allotted moments.

- *Be 'on deadline'*. If necessary, prepare an auto-return message stating your incapacity for email correspondence due to being 'on deadline' with a major project. This may seem a little pompous, but it's effective in letting people know why you may be maintaining email silence. Certainly, I've seen this from editors of periodicals as they approach deadline, so it's surely extendable to other professions – especially since the irritation threshold from people expecting a reply to their email can now be measured in minutes.
- *Avoid long threads*. These can often be conversations, perhaps started by a senior, where no one is now willing to absent themselves. But, in most cases, they're threads to nowhere. Eventually the person not replying gains more kudos than those in the debate, so don't add fuel to the fire with further long emails: it's not cool, it's not efficient, it looks insecure and – in reality – it's no more than a timewaster's charter.
- *Delete threads*. One thread-reduction trick is to try to delete all the emails below the one you're answering – and don't be afraid to update the subject line to make it relevant. Again, some may see this as a control mechanism. Fine – *it is!*
- *Subject lines*. While on the subject of subject lines, always use one and make it as generic as possible (cryptic subject lines are as useless as white space). And always add one when replying to an email without one. Also, try to educate regular emailers to include a subject line. Some people seem oddly reluctant, perhaps worrying they'll be filtered by subject when in fact the opposite is true: after date and name the most common way of searching emails is via the subject line, so without one your email is more likely to be lost.
- *CC's*. When initiating an email, restrict the number of CC's. Sure, this may ruffle a few feathers, but in the right direction – making

you the arbiter of exclusivity (although avoid doing this as a deliberate ploy as it will almost certainly backfire). I've always been tempted to CC in uncle Tom Cobley and all – usually when fishing for praise from seniors or trying to prevent someone else taking the credit for a positive. Yet it's my insecurities that turn me into an avid CC-er, and it's a trait I now actively suppress – not least because it gets me into trouble. Many organizations are highly politicized places and over-CC'ing can lead to fights about why you 'included X' in the email. Unbeknown to you, X and Y are currently feuding, and you've just added to the aggravation and lost two allies.

- *Keep emails short.* Even on important subjects, email length should be kept to a minimum. Longer statements – given as proposals or meeting notes – should be an attachment written in a word-processing document, and only when requested or as an agreed outcome of earlier discussions. Don't generate documents for the sake of it as they'll just irritate. Again, smartphones have had an impact here – forcing sometimes lengthy statements onto the email because attachments are hard to open and even harder to read. Fine, but create a headline within the email – something like 'Meeting Note Below: for smartphone ease'.
- *Indiscretions.* Avoid indiscreet comments – always. Even if replying to a privately sent indiscretion, play it straight. If there's an indiscretion in a thread, be the one that deletes the lower emails to prevent it 'going viral' (even if you agree with the sentiment), although resist chastising others for indiscretions or you'll simply be cut out of future correspondence.

  With respect to your own indiscretions, it's worth remembering that these are most tempting when reacting to an email that's somehow triggered you emotionally. No matter what's triggered you, however – no matter how deserved the target – you'll be handing the recipient dynamite they could throw in your face at a future date. Just think: you may be forced to stay on good terms with that person for the rest of your career in order to avoid them using that indiscretion against you. Unlikely as that now seems, why take the risk?

- *Emotional emails.* And there's an absolute golden rule with any email that's had any sort of emotional impact: DO NOT REPLY FOR AT LEAST AN HOUR and – if possible – longer. By allowing time to pass, the emotions will have dissipated and you'll have started thinking strategically. Remember, your judgement should be focused on your long-term goals, not on reacting to your triggered emotions.
- *Junk email.* This is an easy one, so I'm never certain why people get so exercised about it. If unsubscribing to individual junk mail senders fails (as it often does), simply set up a 'junk mail' folder, assign junk to it as it comes in – with the instruction that this sender is 'always junk' – and repeat the process until the problem goes away. I've been doing this diligently for a year and I've managed to get my inbox down from 250 emails a day to . . . let me see now . . . 240!

  OK, it is annoying – especially when eagerly awaited emails find their way into your now avaricious junk folder.

  If it really bugs you, set up several email accounts and keep one exclusively for key contacts (i.e. don't hand it out to people unless you're certain you want them to email you). An alternative email address restricted to important emails may also help regulate the number of times you look in your inbox, as lowering the expectation of email traffic will reduce ADD-style flitting between your email account and other computer programs.
- *Avoid instant messaging and text.* Such devices compress our communication further – even abbreviating language into a sometimes indecipherable shorthand. While both are developing a more business use – having been championed by teenagers – they should never be used in anger (where they can even make email seem conciliatory).
- *Break office silence.* Finally, there's the need for offices to have a buzz, which email kills – with even adjacent colleagues resorting to email conversations in order not to break the silence. I

hate it. If writing an email to someone within easy talking distance, stop writing and speak to them instead. That's unless they're on a major project and are keen not to be interrupted which, of course, they should have communicated. In our office, we use listening to music through headphones as our signal we're concentrating and would rather not be disturbed. If not wearing headphones, we're fair game for a spoken, rather than written, interruption.

**Get Things Done:** *Email has become our master rather than our servant, so we need to regain control. And we also need to avoid email's many landmines – including over-CC'ing, replying too quickly and too emotionally, and using it as a surrogate for strong verbal communications.*

# 13

# . . . IN MEETINGS

According to Alec Mackenzie (of *Time Trap* fame), the average American manager spends 450–500 hours a year in meetings, which is one day per week. If they're not to overwhelm our schedules, therefore, meetings deserve special treatment. Indeed, the self-help universe has produced a series of books focusing on making this most inefficient activity more, well, efficient. That said, most broaden out to include topics such as decision-making and planning – making the one that manages to stay on-topic valuable indeed.

Writing in *Make Meetings Matter* (2008) communications consultant Charlie Hawkins deconstructs meeting dynamics to offer a strong structure for planning and running meetings. Planning is the key, it seems, with Hawkins offering the four Ps for perfect planning: 'purpose, people, place and preparation'.

## What's our purpose?

'Starting a meeting without a purpose is like starting a journey without a specific destination in mind', writes Hawkins.

He's also insistent that we're honest about the reason for our meeting. It's unproductive to force people to labour under a hidden purpose, he says – perhaps the notion that this is a brainstorming session when the real reason is the organizer's desire for approval on a particular idea. Such dishonesty can generate resistance rather than agreement, says Hawkins, which is hardly a recipe for a productive meeting.

Yet Hawkins also states there's no point holding a meeting without a clear idea of the preferred outcome (we just need to state this honestly). And this is the case even if that preference becomes impossible as the meeting unfolds.

Of course, meetings are often about making decisions – hence the sub-genre's temptation to include this theme in their books. But there's a problem: according to McCormack (in *What They Don't Teach . . .*) decisions in meetings smack of decisions by committee, which are usually poor ones (the camel famously being a horse that was said to have been designed by a committee).

This leaves us in the awkward position that McCormack dislikes decision-making meetings while Hawkins dislikes meetings where any decision has been pre-agreed and the meeting is simply to try to force a consensus. As for *Time Trap*'s Mackenzie – his view is that the core purpose of a meeting is planning and co-ordination, as well as for settling issues involving fairness – 'the kinds of decisions people want debated, not dumped on them', he says.

'Meetings are also best for creative problem-solving, giving recognition, and celebrating victories', he states.

That said, I cannot help thinking all these gurus have missed a core reason for a face-to-face meeting: persuasion. While other uses for meetings – such as catch-ups or mentoring – can potentially be as effective via the phone, only a face-to-face meeting can coax possibly reluctant people to your point of view.

## The people

The next Hawkins 'P' is for people: who to make our 'meeting hostages' as Mackenzie calls them. 'Hostages' is a good word because there are few things more unproductive than being trapped in a meeting we shouldn't be attending.

Too many or too few participants can make a meeting unproductive, so we must consider what group size best fits our purpose. If the meeting is to report information, then there's no reason not to invite everyone affected and only allow wider contribution at the Q&A session after a presentation. Yet, if any form of decision is required, smaller groups are necessary – with the participation list limited, according to Hawkins, to those with a direct stake in the process.

McCormack's view is that a meeting's productivity is 'inversely proportionate to the number of people attending it', adding that 'the vast majority of internal meetings are attended by more people than need to be there'.

He blames this on executives who judge the value of what they say by the number of people forced to listen to them. The other major cause is what he calls the 'left-out factor', in which people judge their importance to the company by the number of meetings they're asked to attend.

*Getting out of attendance*

Of course, this suggests we have a choice regarding attending meetings which, for the majority of meetings, is unlikely to be true. In fact, we may work for a meeting junkie who likes meetings for a whole series of reasons that may not be in our interest (to dump work, to syndicate accountability for decisions, to show off). In this respect, not attending meetings may be our most effective strategy, although this will take foresight and tact.

Mackenzie's suggestions for avoiding meetings include (with some added thoughts of my own):

- Providing beforehand any data or information that may have triggered your invitation. Posted with the cheeky note that this makes your attendance superfluous may just get you off the hook – although it may also mean you're asked to turn up and explain the data (or even lead the meeting!).

- Using project deadlines as an excuse to duck meetings. Although it will need to be genuine, a little exaggeration regarding the time/work pressure should go undetected, especially if the project is for the same person inviting you to the meeting.
- In fact, calling for prioritization regarding projects that are backing up may be enough for them to accept the obvious fact that you cannot make progress on one project while sitting in a meeting – and potentially contributing little – on another.
- And then there's the seniority game, which means replying to the invite along the lines of 'sorry, I have to meet a deadline given by X' (with X being more senior). However, care is required, as your excuse could unleash a politicized power play – with you the pawn to be sacrificed.

## Place is important

Returning to Hawkins's four Ps for planning the perfect meeting, we should next tackle place. This is more important than it seems, states Hawkins. He offers the view that 'the room sets the tone for the meeting. If it's inviting, people will feel better and are likely to be better participants.'

Certainly, it needs to be conducive. Stuck in a windowless room too small for the number and with no refreshments, people will feel anxious and impatient, although this has its upside in terms of helping people come to a decision. Indeed, McCormack goes as far as suggesting some meetings are better held standing up (as is the Privy Council meeting with the Queen – initiated as an aid to brevity) or in hallways – offering the bonus that 'people will be less upset about not being invited'.

Meanwhile, Michael Heppell (*How to Save an Hour Every Day*) has the perfect TV role-model for meetings: *The West Wing*. He observes that, in the White House drama, meetings with President Bartlett have the following characteristics:

- No one is ever late so they always start on time.
- No one dawdles in to the room – there is a state of constant hustle.
- No one starts with small talk – it's straight to the crux of the meeting.
- No one offers refreshments, or starts with a PowerPoint presentation, or distributes papers, or worries about who's taking the minutes.
- No one even sits down – with many meetings taking place in a corridor or even on the move.
- No one says 'we'll park it til next week'.
- No one meanders or fence-sits an opinion. Phrases like 'on the one hand . . .' are rarely heard.
- No one offers to write a meeting note to summarize the discussion.

Of course, this is fiction – but the closer we can get to making this our reality, the more effective our meetings will be.

One last thought on place: why not book a room for 45 minutes, rather than an hour? As Heppell states, most meetings last an hour because that's what's scheduled. Yet, if you scheduled 45 minutes instead (perhaps starting at 15 minutes past the hour to reduce the temptation to take it to the hour), the meeting would only last that long, and remain just as effective.

## Go prepared

And finally in the Hawkins quartet of Ps there's preparation. Of course, an agenda's good but they tend to look naked without a list of at least five items (one of which will be the self-defeating AOB). Yet this isn't the annual general meeting of the West Yorkshire Branch of the Municipal Boilermakers Union, so the most effective agenda will be a short one.

Something like:

| | |
|---|---|
| Meeting | June 1st, 12.15 p.m. til 1 p.m. [an awkward time because people will be hungry – encouraging haste]. |
| Place | Meeting room 10 [the small, windowless one]. |
| Agenda | Next steps on the Johnson bid. |
| People | Jim A, Jane B and John C. |
| Note | Phones off. There will be no refreshments and no presentations. |

Yet the most important aspect of the above is in stating the expected outcome – requiring all preparation by all participants to be focused on *that* outcome. And if Jim, John or Jane want some input into those next steps, they'll need to have their arguments ready (though not in a presentation format).

Hawkins talks of 'ground rules' for a meeting, which should be stated beforehand, although this may come across as pompous or controlling. That said, the agenda above makes it pretty clear that intensity of discussion is the key requirement here, not breadth.

For such discussions, our preparation should be no more than 10–20 minutes spent somewhere quiet jotting down the five or six key points we wish to make. What do *we* want from the meeting, what *must* be discussed, what *has* to be agreed? Again, the warning is to stay on-topic – and definitely avoid criticisms or personal point-scoring. I've seen too many meetings hijacked by someone with a (usually personal) axe to grind, which, for them at least, is far more important than the topic being discussed.

## How do we get what we want?

The trouble with all the above, however, is that it seems so negative, as if the best outcome is neutral – that we've not had our time wasted or we've avoided catastrophe. This is a shame because meetings can be fantastically effective in getting what we want. As stated, I think persuasion is the core function of any meeting. So, if we get the dynamics right, meetings should help us take giant leaps towards our goals.

Here are my own thoughts on generating the meeting dynamics that aid persuasion:

- Don't deliberately sit across from the person you aim to influence. Sure, in a one-to-one you'd look ridiculous sitting side by side. But a seating arrangement involving your team on one side of the table and their team on the other makes it immediately adversarial (making agreement less likely). So mix it up.
- Most tables are rectangular, so avoid sitting at the head of the table – offer that to the person you're meeting: it'll make them feel important.
- In fact, right through the meeting you should give off strong signals that the person you're meeting – even if junior – is important and valued. This is *their* meeting. Indeed, start by complimenting them about something – anything.
- When talking, make good eye contact with those in the meeting room. Don't focus just on the boss – rove around, making strong eye contact with everyone.
- Smile. Be bright and cheerful – and remain so even if the people you're meeting are grumpy. That said, their mood may be deliberate – trying to project gravitas perhaps – which you should respect. Showing professionalism and concern, however, doesn't have to involve a frown. And your cheerfulness may be infectious.
- Offer business cards and read the ones given to you (it's always worth getting a quick handle on job titles and hierarchy). If

handed several, I arrange them in front of me to reflect the seating arrangements, which means they act as aid to name recollection.

- Yes, use their names. But don't overuse them. This is a business meeting between professionals, not a seduction (no matter what the sales gurus tell you). Certainly, first or given names are fine. The days when it was strictly 'Mister Smith' until invited otherwise are over, although anyone who's clearly over 60 may still appreciate this approach.
- End the meeting well. I've been left with some terrible impressions by people simply standing up as a silent indication that the meeting's over. It's an arrogant power play and worth avoiding. It's also unnecessary when a simple white lie such as 'I have a three o'clock, so I have to keep going I'm afraid' is far more effective – especially if we add something positive about what's been achieved.
- If you get what you want, put it in writing as soon as possible – that day preferably. This is where email is now on your side, allowing verbal agreements to be formalized before they've had time to think of the negatives. Be brief, but don't delay – verbal agreements in a meeting mean nothing (and can be a way of getting you out the door). Get it in writing – *pronto!*

> **Get Things Done:** *Follow the four Ps for meetings: purpose, people, place and preparation. Persuasion is the key purpose, the people should be the minimum for effectiveness and the place not necessarily that comfortable (to aid brevity). As for preparation: it's a good idea.*

# 14

# . . . WHEN MANAGING OTHERS

'All careers end in management' is one of my favourite pearls of worklife wisdom – not least because it's (mostly) true. At some point – whether we like it or not – we'll have to instruct juniors. Either that or we'll stay junior – or a freelancer at best – having to cope with the instruction of others.

Of course, there are those that claim to be 'happier among the troops than the officers' – as I used to state. But, certainly for me, I now realize this was not based on my egalitarian convictions. It was due to my inner fear that my authority would be ignored, or disputed, or even laughed at. It was my poor self-beliefs that meant I avoided giving instruction, however I disguised it.

If we want to be productive, therefore, we must learn how to be an effective manager – allowing those beneath us in the hierarchy to work *for us* rather than *against us*. Indeed, get management right and we've just multiplied our potential output. Get it wrong, and we'll have to stand and watch others excel while we're chained to the bottom of the hierarchy.

So where to begin? Well, how about with yourself. We need to step through the mirror and look back at ourselves – noticing the impact we have on other people. Too often, insecure or unproductive people are obsessed with the impact others have on them, which renders them incapable of seeing the impact they have on the team they're trying to lead. This was certainly true for me. My early days as a manager – while deputy, then editor, of a specialist financial magazine – were clumsy to say the least. I was a hopeless manager because I was too fearful that my shallow authority would be undermined by those I perceived as more self-assured.

My fear that I lacked authority meant that, ultimately, I relied instead on winning the sympathy of my charges. For those I perceived on my side, this worked – they'd empathize with my complaints about the 'unreasonable' pressures being placed upon me from above. And they'd try to help, although my authority was immediately discarded in the process. For those I perceived against me, I'd imagine them plotting, and would occasionally throw tantrums in defence against some perceived slight – sometimes even interpreting their bewildered silence as disdain or even ridicule. Indeed, my paranoid reactions became self-fulfilling in this respect.

## The power of delegation

Yet my management of people improved markedly once I'd learnt the power of delegation.

'Delegation is rooted in the essential purpose of management, which is to produce results through people', write US business gurus Richard A. Luecke and Perry McIntosh in *The Busy Manager's Guide to Delegation* (2009).

They see delegation as *the* tool for being an effective manager yet recognize that true delegation is often resisted by overly busy managers, who they ask to take the following quiz:

- Are you so busy you barely have time to blink . . . while your reports seem to have lots of breaks when they can chat and goof off?
- Are your tasks pretty much the same as they were before you became a manager?
- Do your managerial colleagues seem less pressed for time than you?
- Is the idea of taking a few days off a dismal joke?

For those answering 'yes' to any of the above, as I certainly would have done in my early managerial career, the answer – according to Luecke and McIntosh – is to become a good delegator.

Delegation is not just good for you, it's also good for them – helping your team upgrade their skills and competencies, and giving them the opportunity to showcase the confidence that delegation gives them.

Yet many managers fail to delegate effectively, often blaming their charges for their own incompetence. Indeed, Luecke and McIntosh cite the following classic excuses for poor delegation:

- 'I can't trust anybody to handle this. I'll look bad if the job isn't done right'
- 'I can do this better than any of my people'
- 'I'm responsible for what happens here. I cannot delegate that responsibility'.

Certainly, all the above resonates with me, with the middle one often time-based – i.e. 'I can do the job in less time than it will take me to instruct someone else'.

Unfortunately, I see the same mistakes being repeated when I now ask my account directors to manage people, so there's clearly something unnatural about the delegation process (not least the fact it can trigger our insecurities).

Yet delegation is an essential 'managerial competency' according to Luecke and McIntosh. It's at the heart of what management is all about, they state, so anyone managing anybody needs to become a strong delegator.

Luecke and McIntosh offer five steps to strong delegation (with some thoughts of my own).

*Step 1: Determine which tasks to delegate*

As expected, they're keen that we delegate as much as possible – including all execution-based work on projects – so we should perhaps think about what shouldn't be delegated. Team selection is perhaps the key one in this respect. As we see in football, the manager's primary role is to enrol the team and select the players. As much as he's tempted, he should stay off the pitch while the game's underway.

*Step 2: Identify the right person for the job*

We should perhaps stick with the football analogy for a bit, because the manager also determines the positions of his players. This is clearly based on the particular skills of the individuals, and it's his job to observe and calculate those skills to determine where each player will be most useful – obviously looking at it from a team perspective. According to Luecke and McIntosh, we should delegate based on those that can devote the time; are interested in the assignment; understand the background; can handle the job; are reliable; and are 'ready to grow professionally'.

*Step 3: Assign the task*

This is an interesting element in the 'art of delegation' because too much instruction can backfire – destroying their motivation for the job. Extraordinarily, less is more when it comes to instruction, even on major projects. In most cases, those you delegate to will be keen to demonstrate their abilities (if not, you may be delegating to the wrong person).

It's therefore vital that you allow them the room to do so. Too much instruction and they'll view the task as simply following your orders, which will quickly demotivate them. Instead, why not agree (together) a vision of what the result should look like and leave it to them to calculate how to achieve that goal? In most cases, this will have them fully engaged and determined to succeed. And, in the few cases where it doesn't – well, that teaches you something about their interests and engagement in the tasks you need doing.

*Step 4: Monitor progress and provide feedback*

Under-instructing them isn't abandoning them to their fate, however. We should monitor their progress (perhaps at scheduled time points, such as 'in an hour' or 'at the end of the day') and offer constructive feedback. Again, avoid micro-managing as it will simply deflate them. And try not to be judgemental, especially in the early phases of a task when they may have simply misinterpreted the 'vision' for the result.

If coaching is required, this is the point at which it will be revealed, although – again – it should be the minimum to re-establish the vision and ensure they have the tools (mental and physical) for completing the task. However, Luecke and McIntosh are very firm: 'never take back the monkey' i.e. allow a frustrated staff member to slide out of the job, something they may do if your 'monitoring' is too heavy-handed.

*Step 5: Evaluate performance*

This is a key moment, although another minefield for a manager who can easily lose a subordinate through clumsy evaluation – and a further classic mistake of my early forays into management. If work arrived that was not what I needed, I used to immediately explode in anger or frustration, as if their 'incompetence' was a personal insult to my authority. Even if the work was good, it would trigger insecurities – perhaps that they held my authority in contempt.

But I've improved, I hope. For instance, I've learnt that praise is the most undervalued commodity in any work environment. Praise is great: everyone (at least everyone worth employing) is keen to win praise and is motivated by it. I seek praise from our clients, just as juniors seek praise from those they report to. So we should seek to give it by the bucketload when evaluating the tasks of others.

Even if they did a poor job, any feedback will be better received if we can start with the positives – any positives. Then, if calculating what went wrong, we should be careful to avoid evaluating the work based on our emotions (as I used to). In fact, we should take a constructive approach, say Luecke and McIntosh – basing our evaluation on elements such as time taken, quality, or their work's proximity to the original premise.

They also point out common evaluation mistakes, such as the 'halo effect' in which we accept poor work from those that usually produce strong output – something that can also work in reverse (that we're overly-critical of work from those we don't rate). Two other common errors are 'isolated incident bias' in which we condemn someone based on one incident, and 'personal difference bias' in which we 'pass' poor work due to some shared characteristic such as gender or background (something that can also work in reverse).

## The task, the ask and the timing

In *How to Save an Hour Every Day*, Michael Heppell breaks what he calls 'dazzling delegation' down into 'the task, the ask and the timing'. When delegating 'the task' it's important, he says, to make sure it's something your nominee wants to do. If not, you may end up having to take it back further down the line – perhaps with a deadline looming. It may help, says Heppell, if you've something (i.e. another task) you can take from them (in order to free up their time).

In 'the ask' Heppell focuses on one phrase and one word. The phrase is 'I need your help' and the word is 'because'. People are programmed to help, says Heppell, as long as we can offer good cause regarding why.

Finally, there's the timing, in which Heppell is concerned we pick carefully the moment to delegate. If someone looks stressed or overly busy, it may be worth waiting a day or two. And, while this may seem an obvious point, for those that are poor at delegation, it isn't. As stated, good managers are those that understand the impact they have on others. Therefore, how we delegate is important – and that includes the moment we choose to ask for help.

> **Get Things Done:** *Delegation is the most important element of management which, if done well, can multiply your output. Less is more when delegating, allowing your team to flourish through finding their route. That said, agreeing the vision is important.*

# 15

# . . . BEYOND WORK

Getting things done involves far more than what happens with our careers. We can be just as dissatisfied by productivity in our life outside of work. Certainly, we can find ourselves mentally cluttered once beyond the office door – perhaps feeling trapped within social groups that no longer share our values, or stuck with unfulfilling routines, or even burdened by personal responsibilities.

The answer, according to organizational gurus such as Julie Morgenstern (of *Never Check Emails* . . . fame), is to realize that the emotional barriers that may hamper your career pursuits can also act as a drag at home.

Morgenstern's view is that it's possible to blast your way out of this inertia through the adoption of clear ambitions for your home or social life. No less than at work, you need to set motivating, long-term objectives. And, again, the need is for positive goals: pursuing something you want rather than fleeing something you dislike, such as feeling 'lonely' or 'bored'.

Indeed, 'no one lets go of anything without reaching for something else', says Morgenstern, which is equally true in our social or domestic situations as at work, with the obvious corollary that, if we have no goals to reach for, we'll continue to cling on to our past.

## Develop themes for your life

We must develop 'themes' for our personal life, says Morgenstern (writing in *When Organizing Isn't Enough*, her 2008 book on mental and physical decluttering). She cleverly separates them into zones such as finding love, living healthily, expanding boundaries (perhaps through learning or via new physical activities) or even pursing an adventure or seeking 'serenity'.

Of course, all the above can be combined though the adoption of some transformative, theme-based pursuit such as yoga or volunteering. In fact, given that your dissatisfaction may be symptomatic of a deeper mental malaise, the more holistic the theme, the better.

Morgenstern asks that you take a 'big-picture approach' that involves looking at all aspects of your life – not just the empty zone that could be your social life or the fact your personal finances are a mess (see below). They're all connected – offering either a sense of well-being or, more likely, the opposite.

Yet she also asks that we 'keep it simple', which is a plea not to add unnecessary complexity when it could be a decluttering that's required (with too many commitments being at issue, rather than too few). Again, this focuses on the likelihood that a single thread runs through various aspects on your non-work dissatisfaction, which you should try to identify. Perhaps you feel trapped in your current circumstances, or maybe the issue's one of isolation. You could even feel overwhelmed: indeed, it's worth trying to find the one word that best describes your concern – what Morgenstern describes as the 'lens' through which you evaluate your life.

Finally, on themes, Morgenstern insists that you shouldn't 'short-change yourself'. Generate themes that focus on your 'highest aspirations', rather than the minimum you 'feel you can manage'. Whether it's a new activity you want to master (such as playing the piano), or an entirely 'new you' (perhaps moving into the big city rather than commuting from your home town), the theme should be something you strongly desire – as only that will inspire you enough to bring about the necessary changes.

## Points of entry

And, with the theme settled, we're off: via the adoption of Morgenstern's somewhat contrived SHED mnemonic.

- *Separate* all your 'treasures'. This means examining everything in your life – including possessions, actions and habits: and working out what supports your personal progress and what impedes it.
- *Heave* all your 'trash'. Having identified the 'treasures' you wish to keep, you should remove all the possessions, activities and bad habits that prevent change.
- *Embrace* 'the remarkable individual that you are'. Realize you're not defined by objects or interests, or even by the people you know. Embracing an overarching theme is an important part of this transition – giving you the perspective to look beyond your possessions.
- *Drive* 'into the future with vision and hope'. Having unloaded the baggage, you can now reload your existence with the possessions and activities that reinforce your 'theme', though this shouldn't be a headlong pursuit to replace one acquisitive habit with another.

Morgenstern's mental and physical de-cluttering is achieved via 'points of entry'. These can be rooms full of junk, poor habits or unhealthy activities. Indeed, there are 'entry points' in three zones, says Morgenstern: 'physical' (including possessions); with respect to your 'schedule' or non-work commitments; and regarding your 'habits'. In all three, ruthlessness is required, she says, if you're to free-up your free time for potentially transformative pursuits.

Yet some care is required. Jettisoning friends, for instance, can quickly leave us emotionally bewildered, especially if we experience setbacks on our journey towards some social nirvana we've not properly thought through. It may also feel false, and be declared as such by associates, again reinforcing our sense of confusion and even isolation. Yet such caveats simply reinforce Morgenstern's notion of 'treasures', and the fact we should separate all aspects of our life into things that reinforce the 'rut' – which should be removed (or 'trashed' in her parlance) – and things that help us reach a new level, including friends, which we should nurture (see Part Four for more on 'others').

## Tackling financial phobia

Life outside work can generate issues significantly less benign than a cluttered house or empty social life. Our personal finances, for instance, can act as a major barrier to our progress. Indeed, all the above advice denies one crucial and potentially limiting concern: money. If our personal finances are in disarray, such plans will be halted immediately.

Of course, money is a perennial concern for most people. Yet 'financial phobia' – as it's become known – goes much deeper than mere money worries. It's a disabling mental affliction that impacts both our ability to match our spending with our income – either overspending or, just as likely, assuming everything unaffordable – and our competences with respect to long-term planning.

And this is no obscure affliction. Research by Dr Brendan Burchell of Cambridge University claimed that one in five Britons suffers from financial phobia, which he described as a 'mental condition that prevents people sorting out their personal finances'.

According to Burchell, 'financialphobes can be intelligent people who are high achievers in most areas of their lives – they are not irresponsible, feckless or spendthrifts'.

Nonetheless, they've become trapped by the psychological concerns associated with money. Many feel apprehension when having to deal with money matters, while others are simply bored or distracted (resulting in typical ADD-style behaviour). Yet, for as many as 45 percent of sufferers, thinking about financial matters produces physical responses such as classic fight-or-flight symptoms (including a racing heartbeat, the sweats and shaking).

It also afflicts people right across the income spectrum. Certainly it afflicted me, and still does to a lesser extent. I hated anything to do with *my* money. Of course, I worried that I didn't have enough – as most young people do – but it went way deeper than that: as if by peering into my finances I'd be confronting the undeniable truth that I was somehow unworthy.

So what can be done to overcome financial phobia? One problem is that the solutions seem so bland: creating Excel sheets with incomings in one column, expenses in the other, and with rows added for savings or outgoings. Fine – except that's not how we've tackled other areas, so why be so anal when dealing with an area that, at best, bores us and, at worst, terrifies us into denial?

A more philosophical approach is required.

'In your relationship with money, you are the living being and money is your tool', writes personal finance guru Suze Orman in *The Laws of Money, the Lessons of Life* (2003). 'Money does not define you or make you more valuable as a human being.'

## Money is our slave not our master

Orman's advice floats above other works on the subject because she's not interested in the minutia of each transaction: that's your issue, once motivated to do so. She's offering a sympathetic voice – declaring that money is a means to an end, not the end in itself. It's our slave not our master, although it's a slave that demands respect nonetheless.

For Orman, decisions about money must take place within the context of long-term personal goals. Well-documented objectives will have action points, which will have costs. And it's these that must concern us, although we'll be motivated to tackle such concerns only if we've a strong understanding of both the bigger picture, and the immediate and detailed use of our financial resources.

This may seem obvious, although it's already a transformation in thinking for the financially phobic, who'll almost certainly view money, not as a lever for advancement, but as an impediment. To help, Orman offers five rules – or 'laws' – that can act as principles for using money as a tool (with some thoughts of my own).

*Law One* – tell the truth. This isn't necessarily a moral point. Sure, money can turn us all into liars – perhaps using credit to give ourselves the appearance of being successful. But take this too far and we'll be found out or, worse, we'll dig the hole deeper and deeper in order to maintain the pretence. Own up to your financial lies, says Orman, no matter how small. Only once the smoke clears can you look ahead.

*Law Two* – don't live in the past. Your financial life is not about the past or even the present. It's about the future. Organizing your finances, therefore, should be a central element of planning your future goals. Orman pleads that any financial arrangements that prevent you from cutting yourself loose from your past should be dealt with as soon as possible – including any debt overhangs, which should be paid off as soon as possible. That said, past financial errors should act only as lessons for future behaviour, not as a totem for your regrets.

*Law Three* – people are more important than money. You're the most important person in your financial world. Yet this is not a 'because you're worth it' treatise to indulgence. In fact, it's the opposite. It's advising you to listen to your fears – noting that you might not have the risk tolerance for recklessness, or even generosity towards others, that you outwardly claim. Certainly, 'living within your means' is as much about emotion and fear, as it's about finance. Recognize this.

*Law Four* – get your financial priorities straight. Just as you've had to cut off the past, you must secure the present. First, devote financial resources to your immediate needs and obligations:

food, shelter, debt payments etc. Only then can you look at investing in your future. Sure, you can look to economize in order to free-up 'investment capital'. But ignoring current obligations (perhaps by only paying the monthly minimum on a credit card) is simply storing up trouble. Why not see it as a financial version of Maslow's hierarchy of needs, with your self-esteem investments only possible once you've secured lower-order necessities?

*Law Five* – you control your money, not *vice versa*. Many people are condemned to feeling powerless about money, which leads to the erroneous thought that, if only they had more, they'd become empowered. But money doesn't determine your personal worth: you do. Indeed, using money to acquire feelings of self-worth is the realm of the perennially insecure, not least because (unless you're Carlos Slim) there'll always be someone with more money. So *Law Five* involves a mindset change: that power comes from inner strength not outer wealth. And this means that, if we spend money in order to acquire self-esteem, it's simply money down the drain.

**Get Things Done:** *Your home and social life should be treated no differently to your work life. Long-term objectives are required, which allows for a ruthless re-evaluation of social priorities and even possessions. Tackling financial phobia, meanwhile, involves seeing money as a lever for your advancement, not an impediment.*

# PART FOUR

# Other People

# 16

# PERSUASION AND INFLUENCE

We can be the most white-hot efficiency machine ever invented. Without the support or at least the acquiescence of other people, however, we'll hit a brick wall, which will potentially wreck our development – even sending us back to our ineffective worst.

So how do we enlist others in our pursuits? Two schools of thought quickly emerge. Oddly (for modern ears), the first involves conflict. We can force or coerce people. This looks like a highly effective route – so effective, in fact, that most of human history seems to have progressed through war, invasion and subjugation. Even as individuals, many still subscribe to this notion – not overtly, perhaps, but via competitive instincts that force us to think in terms of a win/lose paradigm. I win, ergo, you lose.

Indeed, the continued popularity of Sun-Tsu's *Art of War* is proof enough that many are still persuaded by this school. Sun-Tsu was a Chinese general writing around 2500 years ago, although for many his resonance is as strong as ever. He pervades modern day business thinking simply because so many ambitious men (yes, it's usually men) live either consciously or unconsciously by his code.

Niccolò Machiavelli is another hero of the conflict school of people management. His book *The Prince* at least gets us into the early-modern era (it was written in 1513), although is equally – err – Machiavellian.

In fact, *The Prince* can be summed up in one phrase: the end justifies the means. It's a handbook for power-desperate manipulators – conjuring the deceit, trickery and outright oppression required for success in the Florentine court, or any other workplace environment for that matter.

And modern writers continue the craze. One book in particular makes me cringe whenever I see it being read on the tube: *The 48 Laws of Power* by Robert Greene (written with Joost Elffers in 2000).

This is a fantastically successful book – not least because its laws all contain a nugget of truth. Indeed, that's the problem with all these books: they offer advice from the dark side that's not only true (at least in part), it's highly effective.

Just a brief look at some of Greene's laws illustrates the point:

- *Don't trust allies, but learn how to use enemies.* Out of envy, friends will betray you. So never hire friends – hire enemies. Forgive an enemy and they'll want to prove their loyalty.
- *Conceal your intentions.* If people don't know your goal, they cannot defend against you. Envelope your intentions in smoke.
- *Take credit for others' work.* Others have wisdom, knowledge and endeavour. Use it. But make sure *you* take the credit. No one will remember those who made your success possible.
- *Make others come to you.* Never act first. Never go to the other person's territory. Lure them, seduce them, draw them to you – then attack.
- *Avoid losers.* Emotions are infectious and the unfortunate sometimes draw misfortune towards them. Shun the poor, the unlucky, the unloved and the unhappy.
- *Make people dependent on you.* You must always be needed as it gives you the freedom to act. Keep others dependent – it keeps you in control.
- *Pose as a friend to gather intelligence.* You must know about your rival. So get them to reveal themselves by posing as a friend.
- *Crush your enemy.* When you fight, do not leave your enemy alive to fight another day. Annihilate them – not only in body but in spirit.

- *Cultivate terror through unpredictability.* Make people exhaust themselves trying to figure you out. In extreme cases, volatile changes of mood, temper or plan can empower you as a tyrant.
- *Play the courtier.* The courtier is adept at intrigue, manipulation, image, flattery and flirtation. The perfect courtier looks good and manages to assemble power without seeming to grasp.
- *Keep your hands clean.* You must seem a paragon of civility. So use someone else to do your dirty work. Then find someone else to take the blame.
- *Deal the cards to control the game.* Your victims should be your puppets. Seem to allow others some freedom of choice, but always invisibly control the boundaries.
- *Learn what hurts and use it.* Everyone has weaknesses, vulnerabilities, insecurities, needs or sensitivities. Learn them and exploit them. Inflict or relieve pain as serves your purpose.

Need I go on?

Of course, the veracity of the above statements makes them all the more depressing. Yet there's hope for those desperate to avoid such obnoxious tactics in their pursuit of productivity. When it comes to getting things done, the homilies of Sun-Tsu, Machiavelli and even Robert Greene contain one fatal flaw for their modern application. We have to vanquish our enemy, which is simply impractical in today's working environment. Murder is unacceptable (at least for the sane), which means our enemies are likely to stick around and potentially plot their revenge.

And this makes persuasion a far better option.

## Persuasion is a survival tool

That said, persuasion also has its problems. In *Persuasion* (2005), renowned business coach David Lakhani unravels what he calls one of 'mankind's survival tools'.

'Good . . . persuasion involves understanding the true needs and desires of the person you are persuading', says Lakhani, 'understanding his or her criteria for action, and finally presenting information in a way that is congruent with his or her indicated desires.'

This is a long way from Sun-Tsu or Machiavelli. It's about 'developing consensus through discussion', says Lakhani. There are no dead bodies – quite the opposite. It's aimed at providing a good outcome for all parties – the fabled win-win of management speak.

So where are the problems? In fact, there are two. First, we may not be in a position to persuade anyone of anything. Persuasion requires us to be on the inside of the decision-making process – or at least able to affect it – while we may in fact be an outsider, or a mere recipient of others' orders.

Second – and more importantly – persuasion still focuses on winning. Sure, we're now seeking a win-win, in which we persuade someone that what we offer is what they want. Except – in reality – we're not. We're focused on our own 'win' and using their 'win' as a means of achieving it. This could be manipulative because, in many cases, we'd happily jettison their win if we could achieve our win without it.

Seeing their win as the price for achieving our win (whatever language we use to describe it) renders persuasion, in my view, little better than an acceptable version of war, hence persuasion – for me – remains in the first school for enlisting others in our pursuits.

## Winning influence

The second school involves something far less tangible than either war or persuasion, but something far more sustainable: influence. Of course, influence sounds like a mild or more tepid version of persuasion – but it's far deeper than that. Persuasion is a face-to-face negotiation: an exchange in which you're hoping for victory (perhaps by offering them something they want in exchange). Influence, meanwhile, is a side-by-side collaboration.

Influence makes you a fellow traveller on the same journey – with conjoined objectives. And that makes influence far more powerful than persuasion because you've immediately done something very effective for enlisting others: you've made achieving *their* pursuits your central aim.

Your objectives need to be aligned, of course. So you should search for those you want to influence on the basis of aligned objectives. Once found, however, it's *their* goals that matter. They're the important ones in your quest and, if not, you've simply chosen the wrong person to try to influence.

The great Dale Carnegie tackles this need in probably the most famous self-help book ever written – *How to Win Friends and Influence People* (1936). A crucial tenet running right through the book (what Carnegie calls his 'big secret') is the notion that 'there is only one way . . . to get anybody to do anything. And that is by making the other person want to do it'.

This sounds like persuasion – and is – except there's one key difference. Carnegie has recognized the other person's fundamental wish to be appreciated. To feel important.

He writes that 'the desire for a feeling of importance is one of the chief distinguishing differences between mankind and the animals'.

In fact, he states that it's the key difference that led humans to develop civilization. And while our other wants (such as food, shelter and sexual gratification) are usually fulfilled, it's our desire for importance that drives much of our adult behaviour because it's so hard to achieve – motivating us towards study, success, material acquisition and even criminality in its pursuit.

For Carnegie, someone's sense of importance is the most crucial piece of information we need to discover.

'If you tell me how you get your feeling of importance, I'll tell you what you are', says Carnegie. 'That determines your character. That is the most significant thing about you.'

Making the other person feel important will give you enormous influence, says Carnegie. Of course, this isn't a million miles from Maslow's hierarchy of needs mentioned in Part One, although somewhat completes the picture: having worked out how *our* behaviour is dictated by needs (especially self-esteem), we can step through the mirror and calculate how *others* may be motivated. And how, therefore, we can influence them by aligning with those motivations – helping them achieve *their* goals.

Again, a key difference with persuasion comes into focus. With persuasion we're attempting to give them what we want them to have – by convincing them that they want it. With influence – we're finding out what they truly want, and are finding a way to help them get it, which also removes the notion that this may be manipulative.

## Be liked

Understanding what drives others is only part of the story when it comes to exerting influence, however. You also have to be liked. Being liked is, indeed, powerful – not least because people will want to spend time with you. If you're not liked people will avoid you – and even become suspicious when you offer help.

Unsurprisingly, Carnegie also has some strong advice on how to be likeable.

He has six basic rules:

1. *Become genuinely interested in other people.* This will gain their attention and help develop loyalty.
2. *Make a good first impression.* Smiling is important – it speaks louder than words, says Carnegie. That said, insincere or mechanical smiles can backfire. 'The smile has to come from within', he says.
3. *Remember names.* I'm terrible at this but have learnt that, if I repeat it back a couple of times – very quickly – it can usually

lodge in my memory. This is a critical recall, because if you forget their name they'll assume you've judged them as unimportant – a fatal mistake for winning influence.

4. *Be a good listener and encourage others to talk about themselves.* People find that an exclusive attention on them, no matter what the distractions, is very flattering, which makes it highly effective (more on listening below).
5. *Be interesting.* This is easier than it sounds. We just need to remember that we're talking to an audience (hopefully of one person). We must discern what they find interesting, and stay on that topic. Too often we try to move conversations to what *we* find interesting, or where *we* feel comfortable. Reverse this, and we should be away.
6. *Appreciate the other person.* Carnegie quotes psychologist William James stating that 'the deepest principle in human nature is the craving to be appreciated'. This helps nurture feelings of self-importance.

## Be believed

Next comes credibility. Others can like us but they have to believe what we say for us to have influence. Again, Carnegie has plenty to say on this, (with some thoughts of my own):

- *Avoid arguments.* Arguments make other people defensive. Once in an argument, says Carnegie, you can't win because if you lose you lose and if you win, you also lose.
- *Respect others' opinions.* If you challenge their opinion they'll want to strike back. No matter what the provocation (and believe me I'm often provoked by others' opinions), their view should be respected.
- *Admit when you're wrong.* Making such an admission – quickly – can transform a situation. Far from thinking you're an idiot when you admit a mistake, it gives credibility to the remainder

of your statements and encourages others to admit their own mistakes and weaknesses. Pride, meanwhile, turns us all into liars.

- *Be friendly.* No matter how angry you feel, you'll not win someone over with a hostile or negative approach. So you must suppress such feelings and exude friendliness and positivity – no matter how inwardly hostile you feel towards that person (a feeling you should try to suppress by actively trying to understand them).
- *Get an early 'yes'.* A 'no' response, especially at the start, will mean they develop a 'no' frame of mind throughout the conversation. Evoking agreement in anything helps develop a 'yes' frame of mind that will help when the yes/no dichotomy becomes critical.
- *Let them talk.* Oddly, convincing others usually involves *them* doing the talking. This is especially true when trying to solve problems, as it means you can align your (brief) answers to their needs. In most cases – and with most problems – its unfettered airing is enough for a result to emerge (with you providing the answer simply by listening intently and empathetically).
- *Make it their idea.* That said, no matter how – in your view – the solution was generated, it's a good idea to let it be noted as their idea. Even if subconsciously, they'll notice this and come back to you when further advice is required (and it refutes at least one of Greene's 48 'laws').
- *See it from their point of view.* You must put yourself in *their* shoes – fully and genuinely – to understand *their* needs. This will help see what motivates them, and how you can help them meet their objectives.
- *Show sympathy to their wants.* No matter if you disagree entirely with their premise, say 'I don't blame you one iota for feeling as you do'.
- *Appeal to the other person's nobler motives.* People are idealists at heart, says Carnegie. They like to act out of good motives, even if these hide more selfish sentiments. The appeal, therefore,

should be towards these higher motives – supporting the aims that help them feel good about themselves,

- *Express your view dramatically.* Some drama helps sell an idea, says Carnegie. Certainly, I find this true when selling PR concepts although, in the UK at least, there's a residual reserve that may cause raised eyebrows at overly theatrical demonstrations. In my view, what Carnegie's recognizing is the fact that emotions are powerful in decision-making, and dramatizing our views can help align emotional needs.

## Gaining influence from below

Yet problems remain, of which the crucial one is the fact we may not be in a position to exert influence. We may be too lowly, or ignored, or out of favour. What then?

Well, if we feel powerless, we may first have to put power in its place. Anointed power may look omnipotent but it rarely is. Titles mean nothing because people that are disrespected or misuse their titles generate contempt rather than influence. Indeed, hiding behind a title in order to exert authority is almost certainly an expression of poor influence.

And this makes influence an egalitarian concept in the workplace. Important people can lack influence, while unimportant people can wield it.

So what makes the difference?

This is a conundrum attacked by that now familiar business-excellence pairing Perry McIntosh and Richard A. Luecke in *Increase Your Influence at Work* (2010). The building blocks of influence, they state, are 'trustworthiness, reliability and assertiveness', which have little to do with position.

*Trustworthiness* depends on how we're perceived, they claim. We should openly subordinate our goals to those of the organization and never betray secrets, no matter what the temptations. And we should not sugarcoat information, although we should never lie or exaggerate. In fact, we should try to discern – and stick to – the facts.

Perception also dominates *reliability*. We have to prove that we're dependable, not just state it. Being able to back-up what we say is important, so we must research subjects deeply before expressing an opinion. And we must focus on how things can be achieved, not on the barriers that prevent achievement.

Of course, it can take time for our efforts to be noticed, which is where *assertiveness* comes in. Certainly, we should not conceal our talents, denigrate our achievements or let others bully us into silence say McIntosh and Luecke. We should want to work with others, rather than on our own, and be eager to stand out. Shrinking violets will not gain the influence they deserve, they state.

Indeed, McIntosh and Luecke describe passivity as 'a condition characterized by submissiveness and fear or unwillingness to stand up for one's needs and interests', which will obviously harm our influence. That said, being overly aggressive can be equally destructive, especially with respect to colleagues either alongside or below us in the hierarchy.

We therefore need to find the Goldilocks scenario: neither too passive nor too aggressive. Yet this is a need that can leave subordinates confused, as well as frustrated. To overcome this McIntosh and Luecke suggest six supporting tactics that can help the junior gain influence (with some thoughts of my own):

1. *Earn credit.* Offer favours liberally in the office. Indeed, gain a reputation for doing favours. Don't view it as being a doormat. View it as earning credit. The more one-way favours you execute, the more and more credit you're winning from that individual. One day – someday – you may need to call in that loan, so consider each favour done as adding to your influence pot with that person,
2. *Exploit your expertise.* If you can develop specialist knowledge in anything you have influence. Of course, you should seek to

expand this expertise both out (to other areas) and up (to more important needs),

3. *Build collaboration.* Individuals within organizations, big and small, can quickly develop a 'silo mentality', which means we stay within our role and division – perhaps even guarding it from people we perceive as predators. Yet this is a limiting outlook. We should look beyond such silos – reminding ourselves of the organization's broader goals and focusing on nurturing co-operation between teams,
4. *Develop a network.* Networks are living organisms that are constantly growing and changing. And you should constantly seek to expand yours – in all directions. We don't need to obviously source influence here, just actively bolster the number of people we know in any organization and beyond,
5. *Listen.* Yes, that old chestnut. Yet to yield influence with people you need to understand what concerns them, which may not always be obvious,
6. *Become a 'thought leader'.* This is more about insight than persuasion. McIntosh and Luecke cite Aristotle's view that speakers must understand their audiences' thoughts and feelings, and connect with *their* emotions. With that in mind, you can initiate ideas that – even if rejected – help increase your influence.

Of course, none of this will generate influence overnight. Endurance is crucial – comforted by the fact that, given time and effort and resilience, we *will* become influential no matter what our station.

A cautionary note to end on, however. Although influence takes time to build, it can quickly collapse. Too bold a leap or too clumsy an execution, and we could find our influence whipped away – making it all the harder to rebuild having lost it. Having built influence, therefore, we need to nurture it – and guard it assiduously.

**Get Things Done:** *Enlisting others is vital. Yet coercion is no longer an option, and even persuasion is potentially manipulative. Only by genuinely aligning with someone else's goals can we develop the influence required to ensure their support. Influence, however, is difficult to win but easily lost.*

# 17

# DEALING WITH CONFLICT

Conflict is inevitable. Indeed, if there's no conflict, we may be deliberately avoiding it – perhaps due to fear. In fact, avoiding conflict could be a key reason for our stalled progress, which – far from being a virtue (as it's often portrayed) – makes avoiding conflict a low-level form of self-sabotage.

I hate conflict, which may surprise many people who know me – not least because I can seem continually embattled. But that doesn't mean I like fighting. Just that I'm keen to make progress and often fly into conflict unawares.

This makes me clumsy and negligent. Yet it doesn't mean I should steer clear of tussling with others. It means I should deal with personally-competitive issues more effectively. Certainly, when I've dealt with conflict well, I've been able to recruit people to my cause. But when I've poured petrol on the flames, I've annoyed people unnecessarily – causing me to lose battles as well as collect enemies.

## Don't be a conflict coward

Dealing with conflict is therefore an important part of getting things done: a skill we cannot ignore in our pursuits. But what if we are what lifecoach Tim Ursiny calls a 'conflict coward'? How can we cope – and even prosper – from something we're so afraid of?

In his popular 2003 book *The Coward's Guide to Conflict*, Ursiny confirms that our hatred of conflict is, indeed, fear: of the unknown, of losing, of being humiliated, of being manipulated by others. This makes our only rational-seeming response a fight-or-flight choice, he says, with all the negative consequences that entails.

'True conflict cowards know that fearing conflict is not simply a matter of choice,' says Ursiny. 'In other words you can't just decide one day not to be afraid.'

So we need to analyze fear. To understand it.

Ursiny points to 10 fears:

1. *Fear of getting hurt.* This can result in a literal fight-or-flight reaction – with our fears triggered and our responses heightened just as if meeting a predator in the primeval forest.
2. *Fear of being rejected.* Almost as basic as our fear of physical pain is our fear of emotional pain, usually due to rejection. At root, many conflicts are triggered by such fears.
3. *Fear of losing a relationship.* A more exaggerated form of fear of rejection – especially for those who develop dependencies on particular individuals or arrangements. Of course, creating conflict here can be self-fulfilling.
4. *Fear of provoking anger.* This may come from people brought up in angry houses or, paradoxically, where anger was suppressed despite the underlying conflicts. And our fear may be based on avoiding angry reactions from others, or from triggering our own loss of control, with all the negative consequences this will almost certainly generate.
5. *Fear of being called selfish.* Selfishness is a negative trait and few people welcome the label, however justified the charge.
6. *Fear of saying something wrong.* Fear of 'putting our foot in our mouth', as Ursiny puts it – especially with significant others or seniors at work – can lead us to not react when perhaps we should.
7. *Fear of failure.* A simple one this – we fear that, if we get into a conflict (or any other form of competition), we'll lose. What

then? Humiliation, withdrawal, bitterness: all consequences – many people conclude – that are worth avoiding through passivity.

8. *Fear of causing pain.* Conflict can inflict pain, which we may be desperate to avoid. Indeed, this may be one of the most common causes of conflict-avoidance – not wanting to visit the consequences of the fight onto others, especially when the other person is a loved one.
9. *Fear of success.* Just as failure can bring fear, so can success. If we win our battle, then what? We'll 'own' the consequences of any victory, which may be a strong reason for ducking the battle.
10. *Fear of closeness.* Intimacy scares many people. Avoiding conflict could, bizarrely, be a form of avoided intimacy. We'd rather stay out of it and keep our distance than step in and – potentially – commit to a situation or person, even if just in opposition.

## The fruits of dealing with conflict

Ursiny empathizes with our fears, of course. But he also suggests a focus on the upside – what he considers the 'fruits of learning to deal with conflict'.

These include:

- Understanding how conflicts arise, which can help us better judge when avoidance is the stronger option.
- Being able to calm others within a conflict.
- The ability to pull-up or confront others without ramping up the conflict or hurting others.
- Being able to manage conflicts with colleagues both above and below us, as well as alongside us, in the hierarchy.

So what's the magic ingredient that helps us overcome our fears, while still being able to cope with conflict and potentially come through it well? According to Ursiny, it's listening. Ursiny's convinced: in all circumstances, listening is a better way of solving conflict than talking, especially if we can apply the right style of listening.

He lists five types of listening:

1. *Listening with appreciation.* Ursiny tells us to relax and enjoy the feeling of listening, as if hearing a piece of music.
2. *Listening with empathy*, which helps others express what they feel thanks to our encouragement and moral support.
3. *Listening comprehensively.* Our aim here is to assimilate knowledge or instruction, perhaps when trying to decide the right course of action.
4. *Listening with discernment.* Here, we're the detective or the journalist getting to the bottom of something – trying to make sense of events and sequences.
5. *Listening to evaluate.* Do we have a remedy for the problem? Indeed, should we take action at all? Listening in this instance is a little more prejudicial. We have an answer but need to assess whether it's right.

Get our listening right, says Ursiny, and we're turning conflictual situations into a positive experience. As to knowing what type of listening to employ, the answer is obvious: we should listen for the clues.

## Classic conflict errors

Certainly, conflict dogged my early career. I was just too insecure, too fearful, too defensive. Even now, I can find myself making some classic errors – including:

- *Responding emotionally.* Just about every fight I've ever been in has triggered an emotional response. In fact, many became conflicts purely because my reactions were too emotional.
- *Focusing on the impact on <u>me</u>.* Another classic error. It was always *my* feelings that mattered, meaning I'd no idea how my actions and statements were impacting *them*. No wonder it so

often ended in trouble – with both sides quickly in their corners shouting 'listen to me'. Only now can I see that, while both sides were always responsible, it was *my* responses that made things worse.

- *Not caring about the details.* Facts matter. They're usually at the root of the problem, and often the way out (once the emotions have dissipated). So why would I so often dismiss the details? Was it because I didn't have a strong handle on the nitty-gritty, or worried the facts would show me in a poor light? Too often, I fear, this was the case.
- *Prejudging people and situations.* Walk into any negotiation with a prejudice – perhaps that all men are selfish – and you'll almost certainly have it confirmed. Yet that's all you'll achieve because that's all you've set out to achieve. This is a common failing for the conflicted, and explains why the two genders battle away generation after generation. Yet my prejudice often went deeper: it involved prejudging their view of me, which is an inverted form of prejudice (prejudging that I'm the victim) – and often a self-fulfilling one,
- *Looking for solutions that prove the prejudice.* Wanting the result that proves our prejudice is not uncommon. For instance, if a project goes in a direction we dislike, it's hardly unusual for us to wish it ill, as well as gain some satisfaction when it goes wrong. Yet what about engineering such a result? That takes conflict to a different level, although – I must confess – that's been my ambition on occasion.

## Cognitive dissonance

So what's going on in my head? Well, apart from all the emotional baggage of my childhood, one problem – according to many social psychologists – is what's known as 'cognitive dissonance', a notion explained by Stanford psychologist Leon Festinger in his 1957 work *A Theory of Cognitive Dissonance*.

However acquired, I'll have developed strong beliefs, which have become the prism through which I evaluate the complexities around me. Yet these beliefs are sometimes challenged – perhaps by people with different beliefs presenting evidence that contradicts mine. Strong evidence will discomfort me – perhaps throwing me into a state of 'cognitive dissonance', in which doubt and confusion have polluted my previously pure belief system. If I accept the evidence, I'm potentially undermining further core beliefs, which could bring the whole edifice down. So, instead, I find ways to make the new evidence consistent with my existing beliefs.

Of course, this is often by refuting it, which will only deepen the conflict. Or it may be by looking critically at the person – or even the organization – offering the evidence (which explains why media organizations are so routinely accused of bias), all of which goes to prove how disturbing cognitive dissonance is to our sense of self.

## Bringing it to work

So is there a practical way out? According to family therapist Sylvia Lafair in *Don't Bring It to Work* (2009) there's at least a way in – usually by recognizing the role *we* play in generating conflict.

As with other writers, she states that the belief systems we hold in the workplace are likely to be generated by our situation at home.

'Conflict runs rampant in the workplace because of our natural and universal tendency to bring our families with us to work', she writes.

This is true even in 'healthy families' in which members take on invisible roles such as the 'good girl' or the 'smart one' or the 'joker', says Lafair. Indeed, we can even find these roles comforting – our natural state perhaps – meaning we'll seek them out when thrown into a new group or situation (such as a new job). And while, for those from healthy families, this is unlikely to generate conflict – quite the opposite – the chances are that the person getting into fights hails from an 'unhealthy family', in which those early-life roles can encourage conflict.

So if we accept that our backgrounds may have done some damage – but we're also aware of our practical need to reduce, rather than inflame, office conflict – what can be done? Lafair offers the following suggestions for reducing the flammability of conflictual situations (with my usual added thoughts):

- *Striving for balance.* Too much openness can lead to chaos and anxiety, says Lafair. Rules are a good alternative, although – where possible – these need to be agreed. That said, seniors that hide behind rules can also create conflict.
- *Promoting expression.* Not wanting to be labelled troublemakers, workers – and even entire workplaces – can suppress issues. Meanwhile, other workplaces can seem like a soap opera of continuous drama. A happy medium, says Lafair, is a structured setting (such as a weekly meeting) for people to raise issues.
- *Reducing stress.* Office tensions are often created from external pressures such as too much or too little work, or because layoffs are in the air. It's important that organizations recognize these issues and try to reduce their impact on the team. Of course, such pressures may be forcing underlying tensions to the surface.
- *Structuring communications.* Emotional responses often emerge from frustration – sometimes because we feel we cannot express ourselves within a formalized structure. Teaching communications skills – perhaps by holding workshops – can help teams express themselves in an unemotional way, says Lafair.

## Choose to defuse

Lafair's idea of a communications workshop is a sound one, though hardly practical for individuals struggling away with their own issues. If we're in conflict with a senior person or significant other, for instance, we may face high stakes, stubborn opponents and few resources for 'conflict workouts'. What then?

For a start, we can 'choose to defuse' – as recommended by conflict resolution specialist Sybil Evans in *Hot Buttons* (written with Sherry Suib Cohen in 2000).

'It's your call', she writes. 'Attitude is a choice. If you choose to react to your own pushed buttons with an attitude of blinding anger, you'll get nowhere. If you understand why people incite your rage and what you need to do to turn off your (and their) anger, you'll react another way and find a solution.'

Evans offers a five-step formula, which she thinks applicable to nearly all conflicts. She also thinks the steps reasonably obvious, which should help make them 'second nature'.

These are (with some thoughts of my own):

1. *Watch the play.* We need to remove ourselves from the action – standing back and becoming the observer, as if watching a play from the stalls of a theatre. Even if done for just a fleeting moment, the view of us as one actor in an unfolding drama should give us perspective and help restore mental balance.
2. *Confirm.* No matter how righteous you feel, it's worth remembering Festinger's point on cognitive dissonance in order to realize that they, too, are discomforted by the evidence presented. Confirming that their feelings are valid – even if you disagree with them – helps at least prevent fuel being added to the fire. It disarms them by signalling a readiness to listen.
3. *Get more information.* The point here is not to use facts against them, or to support your own beliefs, but to elicit the background that led them to this point of view. Open-ended questions can help – giving the other person the opportunity to answer the question in different ways. Indeed, it's important to avoid the conflictual courtroom style 'just answer yes or no' questions, which will make people feel cornered.
4. *Assert your own interests.* So far, we've been focused on understanding *them*. But *our* views count and, having given them the

room to explain their side, we've won the moral authority to insist our side is also aired. That said, it's a good idea to respond to the cues they've offered, which accepts them as valid. Indeed, if we can offer some form of agreement with them – even if it's the weak 'I can see why you're upset about this' – we're at least showing some alignment, from which we can – gently – assert our feelings, interests and needs.

5. *Find common ground for a solution.* The need now is to find a mutual way forward, involving agreed 'next steps' or promises to moderate behaviour. Collaboration is a good word to describe a more collegiate way forward, with communication a key means of achieving it. Indeed, communication is often the key issue, which makes it possible to both look forward – agreeing to pre-agree future action; and back – agreeing that what went wrong was mostly down to poor communication (a low-blame way out that allows both parties to move on).

> **Get Things Done:** *Workplace conflict is often a result of our fears, which means we avoid conflicts when we should instead learn to deal with them effectively. Listening is a key tool, as is recognizing the insecurities that may drive our responses. Finding genuine common ground is possible, especially if we focus on collaboration and communication.*

# 18

# DEALING WITH THE FAMILY

This chapter divides into two: dealing with the family we're born into (a more psychological than practical pursuit for many adults); and dealing with the family we create (very much a practical quest in terms of generating efficiency enhancing harmony).

Of course, we start with the family we're born into because that's what world-renowned family therapist Virginia Satir calls the 'factory' where people are made. The personality that emerges in our 'family of origin', she states, can stay with us our entire lives.

According to Satir, we're hardwired at this point, especially with respect to the roles we develop within our original family; roles that remain vital when considering our immediate reactions to trigger-situations.

These roles emerged while trying to cope with the environment we confronted from our earliest sentient moments. In dysfunctional families – perhaps caused by an ill-suited marriage or where other issues create conflict – Satir's view is that five common roles become apparent, especially when stressed.

These are (with some added thoughts of my own):

- *The 'blamer'* – who finds fault and criticizes. This is sometimes the stronger adult, perhaps because they feel they should be in a better place.
- *The 'computer'* – a non-affectionate intellectual. Often a child, they're opting out of the situation by focusing elsewhere.

- *The 'distractor'* – who stirs things up. Perhaps the weakest child, they're looking to shift the blame by generating conflict elsewhere.
- *The 'leveller'* – who is open and honest. Again, often a child – perhaps a favourite of one of the adults.
- And finally *the 'placator'* – an apologetic people-pleaser. This could be the weaker adult, desperate to contain the conflicts.

## The Satir Model

According to Satir, only *the leveller* exhibits healthy self-esteem, with his or her inner feelings matching their external communications. Otherwise, the roles are a mask – a means of coping with a deeply dysfunctional situation, especially at stressful moments when immediate reactions are triggering emotional responses.

Such roles allow the family to function, says Satir, although at the cost of each individual's 'authentic self'. In fact, according to Satir, even the communications between family members can lack authenticity – with 'presenting issues' or surface problems acting as a surrogate for the real, deep, and potentially-unsolvable rifts within the family.

Satir was speaking from deep personal experience. The eldest of five, she was brought up on a Wisconsin farm with an alcoholic father – her insight into the dysfunction around her rendered more acute by the fact she lost her hearing due to illness. And, since the 1970s, the 'Satir Model' has become hugely influential in family psychotherapy, to the point she's often referred to as the 'mother of family therapy'.

Certainly, I can see myself in her model (as *the distractor*), and I can also see how such a role has shaped both me and, importantly (according to Satir), my reactions to stressful situations. I become defensive: feelings of guilt mix with a sense of injustice, and an inner feeling of uselessness – meaning my initial instinct is to try to shift the blame. Of course, this rarely works, so my next tactic is to run away – withdrawing from what I perceive as a painful situation or from a scene that could turn negative.

And my productivity is majorly damaged from such a role. For me, pressure – any pressure – results first in an attempt to outsource the problem and, second, a desire to flee or bury my head. Little wonder I was so dysfunctional as a child and young adult, and no wonder my pursuits so often ended miserably.

## Self-worth is a birthright

Given that we're now adults – and ones lacking a time-machine capable of going back to produce a better result – how can we move on from such a disastrous outcome? Satir makes the following suggestions (again, with some thoughts of my own).

- *Recognize what's happened.* The simple realization that we're a product of a dysfunctional family 'factory' helps remove the guilt and undermines our self-loathing.
- *Know our rights.* As stated, there's no going back. But Satir says we must 'accept self-worth as our birthright'. Only then can we move towards fulfilment.
- *Develop love and acceptance.* This is the most potent healing force in any dysfunctional family, says Satir – so we must foster it, no matter how hard it seems.
- *Commit to honesty and openness.* Especially when communicating with others, we must build basic, positive, emotional connections with our family – even if, at first, we meet resistance.
- *Build our own 'healthy' family.* A key need is to use our self-awareness to build our own family, based on reciprocal displays of affection as well as love and positive regard. Such dysfunction must *not* bounce down the generations.

For her part, Satir fostered close and compassionate relations with her patients – mimicking the dynamic she wanted them to adopt with their families (and may have been lacking in their childhood). Forgiveness was crucial, she considered, although true forgiveness is a huge fence to climb – especially if we feel that the original family members haven't accepted their need for change and continue to act as before.

In fact, this is a likely scenario. Positions are just too entrenched, too raw (no matter what the distance in time) for those roles to completely disappear in nearly all dysfunctional-family situations.

How to respond?

While I need reminding of this myself on occasion, I always make the same statement:

'Realize – *you* are the grown-up now.'

By this I mean that, in childhood, we had no choice when it came to the reactions we developed and the roles we played. But – with the self-awareness of adulthood – comes choice. We now have control over how we react – if not initially (due to being triggered) certainly within a short enough time to prevent situations from being run down the same old dysfunctional routes.

In fact, it's your duty to react well. If others have not developed your self-awareness, fine. That puts you in charge. Or, in Satir-speak, it makes you *the leveller*.

## Developing insight

What has all this got to do with getting things done? Plenty. Outsourcing blame or harbouring resentment towards key family members is one of the most disabling traits possible for our effectiveness as an adult. It's as if we're imprisoned inside our adolescent self – stuck under the duvet or slouching lethargically around the house. Sure, we can make progress, but the moment we're challenged or things take a negative turn – *wham*! – back we go under our mental duvet, blaming mum or dad for the crap way they raised us.

Of course, it would be easy here to say 'get over it' or 'grow up' or demand that we 'look to the future'. But that just adds self-loathing to the pot – mixed with guilt for continuing to harbour such feelings and, indeed, being unable to forget the past.

No, we need something much more powerful than censure. We need insight.

'The key to changing the impact of our past on our present is not suppression of reality but insight', writes Oliver James in *They F*** You Up*, '[this means] being able to picture ourselves, to analyze what we are like, to see ourselves as others do, to evaluate our motives.'

James is going beyond understanding. It's not good enough to simply comprehend why we react this way, he says – most likely based on our family history. The insight comes in actually seeing the impact our reactions have on others, as well as ourselves, and in having the presence to catch ourselves mid-action – not to stop the immediate and emotional reaction but to halt the negative consequential actions this may trigger (which can include a stubborn refusal to act).

What's crucial to insight is having what James calls a 'surge of comprehension' – between past pain and present behaviour – while *in the moment*: or at least quickly enough for us to accept that, however triggered, we don't have to flip the switch and act according to some pre-determined script.

Insight this strong doesn't come to us in some great flash of enlightenment, says James. It has to be rediscovered several times before it sinks in that it's our past dictating our reactions – as well as the realization we have a choice whether we allow it to dictate our subsequent actions.

Yet James is concerned that such insight doesn't evolve into blame.

'The most important insights concern how we were cared for by our parents in early life,' he says, 'but it is vital that this should not entail blaming them.'

At this point James cites Philip Larkin's famous poem, which begins: '*They f*** you up, your mum and dad*' – noting that the second verse begins: '*But they were f***ed up in their turn*'.

They had it too, which makes blame inappropriate, says James. Worse – blame destroys our insight, which is understanding without blame. It is true understanding: from every angle.

'Blame means we are still feeling rage,' says James, 'unable to exorcize it through self-awareness. What our parents did to us is not digested; we are simply continuing to experience them as, even now, maltreating us. They live on inside us.'

Hence my plea to realize that *you* are now the grown-up – dealing with *their* hurt and *their* damage – whether this be your parents (or other carers), siblings, aunts or grandparents; and whether they've any understanding or not of what happened and why (in fact especially if they continue to lack such an understanding).

Such insight is a huge leap, in my opinion. It removes the mental shackles. It clears the fog. More than any other single transformation, insight unleashes our potential as a productive grown-up – willing to source and execute objectives-oriented pursuits rather than find excuses not to act. Of course, you may encounter the old reactions or the former roles, but that should simply intensify your insight – a comprehension you should resist throwing in their face (which is no more than an articulate form of blame).

## The family we create

With the pain understood, if not removed, perhaps we can at last use our insight to face the future, as well as look at things from a more practical standpoint.

Of course, this should be through the medium of the family we create. A family, what's more, that must join us on our journey towards strong productivity. Yet progress in our career pursuits can harm our family situation – generating a whole new store of issues that, if not tackled, can end up costing us more than we gain.

Certainly, when it comes to getting things done, generating a strong work ethic can alienate our family. At least that's the case if we're clumsy. If we're skilful, however, it's far from true – the difference being how we inject balance into the equation.

In their empirical study, *Work and Family – Allies or Enemies* (2000), Stewart D. Friedman and Jeffrey H. Greenhaus conducted extensive research into business school graduates in order to highlight the struggle many professionals face when trying to balance work and family life.

The two roles can seem mutually exclusive – each hurting the other – if we fail to manage the balance between them. Yet, interestingly, Friedman and Greenhaus found very different priorities between men and women when it came to coping with the pressures. With women, the balance tips towards the family or marriage – meaning they can find themselves limiting their 'career advancement opportunities' for the sake of family life. With men, however, the difficulty is in participating fully in family life due to the pressures of work.

Nonetheless, Friedman and Greenhaus insist that, for both sexes, it's 'possible to have both a fulfilling career and a satisfying family life, but it requires balanced involvement in both these spheres'.

'Having a life is not so much an issue of time,' they state, 'as it is a matter of managing the psychological interweaving of work and family and of capitalizing on the assets careers generate.'

## Work and families can be allies

For me, a key strength of Friedman and Greenhaus's work is that it's research based – crunching the numbers and reporting 'what is', rather than offering 'how it should be' advice, which can seem unrealistic.

And their research produced six clear themes (with some added interpretation).

1. *Working mothers have it tough.* It's perhaps no surprise that the group most at risk of suffering 'career penalties' when

trying to balance work and the family are working mums. More than men, they feel forced to make trade-offs in order to maintain family life, so they spend time on children's activities and adjust their working schedules to suit. This makes motherhood a career liability, while their research found that fatherhood was a career asset – giving dads more authority or gravitas at work, which helped them achieve more.

2. *Work and families can be allies.* Yet the two needs can be mutually enriching, state Friedman and Greenhaus. Certainly, men pursuing successful careers tend to feel better about their families, while working mums can find work mentally and emotionally supportive. Of course, support from partners contributes to this work-family alliance – and employers need to play their part. Indeed, their research found that, although working mums spend less time at work, their job performance in no way differs, and – if the flexibility's reciprocal – their loyalty to the company increases.
3. *Time is not the major issue.* Interestingly, time is less of an issue than first thought. Parents can organize their time efficiently to deal with both roles. However, a key concern here is what Friedman and Greenhaus term 'psychological interference', which reduces family satisfaction. Certainly, my kids sense when I'm too preoccupied to play with them properly – perhaps with too little 'headspace' (as my wife calls it) dedicated to my family even when I'm physically present.
4. *Authority on the job is essential.* The demands of an unreasonable boss can wreck attempts at a work-family balance, as parents are forced to dance to his or her tune. Friedman and Greenhaus's research found that the more autonomy an employee can win, the better able they are to get the right balance.
5. *Women may be better adapted for the future.* While women are the most pressured in the family situation, they're also the best adapted for the future needs of employers, say Friedman and Greenhaus. Employment is changing: the time and

geography of work are becoming far more flexible – something that women are more willing to embrace than men, who tend to prefer a mental and physical work/life divide.

6. *Kids are impacted.* Children suffer when parents are too focused on their careers. Many develop social or behavioural problems due to their parents' psychological absence.

## The joy of juggling

Of course, research is all well and good. But what's to be done? As ever, I searched the texts for an answer, before realizing I had plenty of experience in this area, not least from my numerous and repeated mistakes.

Here are a few of my own thoughts on juggling career and family.

- *Juggle one ball at a time.* When at work be at work, with a fierce concentration on career-enhancing projects and endeavours. But why not give the family the same intensity? Don't just flop in front of the TV or down a glass of wine: switch hats (literally if it helps). My best family time comes when I arrive home and unwind with a pillow fight with my boys, or a game of football. They love me for it, and get cranky with me when I'm 'just too tired' or 'need to talk to mummy'.
- *Get work out of your head.* We're back to 'headspace' here, because there's no point being with your family while your mind's lost on some work project or problem. This is a major concern for me – and a big cause of tension with my wife. Yet I've found a way to switch off by:
  - planning for the next work session before I break,
  - writing the plans down,
  - keeping a small notebook with me in case thoughts and ideas 'pop up' (once on the page I can forget them), and
  - developing, and executing, family objectives . . .

- *Develop family objectives.* In *7 Habits . . .* Covey's timetable divides the week into waking hours that should be fully utilized. Yet (as mentioned in Part Two) the timetable also has a column for roles – CEO, father, son, husband etc. – with a space for weekly goals under each role. Why not fill it in? My father role this week was to start a Playmobil Olympics (though we only managed three events due to competitor boycotts!). The previous week – as Guy Fawkes night approached – I decided to teach them some English history (which included a trip to the Museum of London).
- *Use the timetable.* In fact, Covey's timetable is a fantastic tool because it allows us to schedule our entire week hour-by-hour. When busy, it's worth using because it kills the guilt that – when with the family or working – we should be working or with the family. Schedule the time for work, of course, but also schedule time for the family.
- *Saturday morning's best.* Sometimes, weekend work is unavoidable. So, I've learnt a new discipline: using Saturday morning as if it's a normal working day. If left alone, I can get my work done by lunchtime, which leaves me mentally free to indulge my family for the rest of the weekend. Leaving it until Sunday night, I've noticed, creates a mental cloud over the entire break. And, before mums jump in and shout 'that's easy for you to say', my wife now counts my weekend working as 'credit' – meaning I have to occupy the kids while she goes shopping, meets friends, or works on one of her projects.

## Juggling productivity with our significant other

Of course, many people reading this book have yet to venture down the family path. Many may simply be trying to juggle a partnership with a significant other. And, without the bonds that come with parenting, partnerships can become strained when we suddenly 'get productive'. If one partner adopts intense goal-oriented endeavour – perhaps after reading a self-help book on strong productivity – the other may feel they're 'losing them'; mentally if not also, after a time, physically.

One problem is the way in which the different genders handle stress. According to John Gray, in his classic work *Men Are from Mars, Women Are from Venus* (1992), women relieve stress by talking about it and by exploring their feelings. Discussions quickly broaden beyond the immediate problem, with her stress relieved when she feels her partner is listening and understands. Yet men sometimes receive this as criticism or blame. They feel she's looking to him to 'fix' a situation that's somehow his fault, and they can become defensive.

While women reach out, men back off. Stress turns men inward – retreating to their cave, perhaps to brood on their issues. He may also seek diversions such as going for a drive or watching TV (or, if in a destructive cycle, drinking or eating too much). Certainly, his reactions make him unresponsive, which leaves his partner feeling 'shut out' or rejected.

'Just as a man is fulfilled through [privately] working out the intricate details of solving a problem,' writes Gray, 'a woman is fulfilled through talking about the details of her problem.'

The key need, says Gray, is to realize that men are, in fact, from Mars while women do, indeed, hail from Venus. They speak and act differently. And they have to learn to speak the others' language if they're to give each other the room and support required to make progress while managing to maintain a loving relationship.

As with parenting, a key need to be 'in the zone when in the zone' – that is, to be mentally as well as physically present in the relationship, no matter what the pressures elsewhere. Time scheduling helps, of course, but so does interpreting the different ways men and women need love. According to Gray, to feel loved, men desire 'trust, acceptance, appreciation, admiration, approval and encouragement'. Meanwhile, women need 'caring, understanding, respect, devotion, validation and reassurance'.

'We mistakenly assume that if our partners love us they will react and behave in certain ways,' says Gray, 'the ways we react and behave when we love someone.'

## Both men and women keep score

It's also worth noting that both men and women keep score, says Gray – though in different ways. Men feel that big scores should follow big gestures such as buying her a new car. Yet the car will win him a single point – no more than a small gesture such as an unsolicited hug. So the need is to continually score points rather than offer the occasional 'grand gesture'.

Men score differently – usually when they feel loved or appreciated or admired, or when they win her approval. They also score more negatively – perhaps when criticized or when they feel rejected.

Given that Venus and Mars are so far apart, is there any hope for our relationship when it comes to forging strong productivity? From my reading of Gray's classic book – interpreted for the newly motivated – I'd offer the following small insights.

- *Learn a common language.* Couples must learn to understand the other's language but must also generate a *lingua franca* involving tolerance, understanding and – above all – strong communication. Talking helps her, approval helps him, and affection helps you both. So invest in each other's needs.
- *Include them.* Any new endeavour will be far easier to achieve with the other's support. So tell them about the 'new you' and what you want to achieve. Chances are, they'll be excited and keen to help. Yet they may fear losing you to your work, so you'll need to reassure them – perhaps by bringing them on board . . .
- *Give them a role.* Why not integrate them into the project – not just a passive recipient of information but a key adviser or participant? Give them a role – and make it something that

works right through the process, not just at the beginning. And make it meaningful.

- *As soon as possible, communicate your needs.* When things are becoming stressful or time hungry, warn your partner. Give notice, because if they only find out from your absence or moods they'll feel excluded. For men, this may mean leaving the cave – even if you return after some strong communication. For women, it means lovingly but clearly stating your needs – not expecting the man to somehow intuitively know (sorry, he doesn't possess your equipment in this respect!).
- *Keep the gestures coming.* Finally, remember the point scoring and keep piling on the gestures. Don't switch them off because you're distracted or busy – or because you feel they'll make no impact. If anything, add more, as this is when you most need to build up your credit.

> **Get Things Done:** *The roles we acquire from our birth family can stay with us throughout our lives and dictate how we react to trigger-situations. This can disable our progress until we develop 'insight', which includes moving beyond blame. With our own families, we need to be time-disciplined and 'in the zone when in the zone'. Meanwhile, couples need to learn a mutual language.*

# CONCLUSION

## 'IT'S ALL CHAOS'

In Part One, visualization was flagged as an important tool for goal setting. Indeed, it's such a key instrument it's recommended by pretty much the entire self-help universe – from mainstream psychologists to the wackiest of fire-walking motivational Svengalis. Given this – and despite some recent criticism that visualization can make you complacent (an unlikely outcome for the insecure in my view, although a potential danger for procrastinators) – it seems a legitimate way to end our journey towards productivity.

However, the aim here is not, as previously, to imagine our desired future. Instead, we need to visualize ourselves going back in time – in fact, by 10 or even 20 years – in order to confront the young and ineffectual person we once were.

If we imagine that meeting – and can get him or her beyond the shock of coming face-to-face with their older and wiser self – what advice would we offer to aid their conversion into the productive and successful person we know they want to become?

In fact, the exercise isn't as daft as it sounds because, the chances are, the lessons we'd like to impart remain relevant for our present and future, though we may have so far failed to articulate them. So, here's our chance. That said, life-coaching our more youthful self is a deeply personal activity – meaning there are no uniform answers.

For illustration purposes only, therefore, I write mine below – the 10 things I wish I could now say to the younger me.

1. *Take responsibility.* There's no white knight just over the horizon: sorry. So please stop thinking you're going to be rescued. Yet, far from being a disaster, this truth – that you're on your own – is good news. It means you must plan your own escape from the mental prison you seem to occupy. It's also worth remembering that, even if the white knight did show up, he'd most likely be pursuing his own self-interests, which perhaps includes you as one small cog in *his* big wheel (a position you'll resent once you realize he's lied to you). You – and only you – are the guardian of your own self-interest. Remember that.
2. *Stuff happens.* Boy, do lots of things go wrong. In fact, things go wrong all the time. But just as many things go well – if not more. And what goes wrong only seems so bad at the time. These 'disasters' rarely make much difference, and any damage is usually easily repaired. In fact – amazingly – many of the problems end up being blessings in disguise. This isn't being fatalistic or retrospectively rational: it's true. So, enough with the anxiety – OK?
3. *React better.* In fact, when things went wrong – and got worse – it was nearly always down to your reactions. You couldn't get on top of your emotions and that made things seem – and on occasion become – worse. How to react better? Try writing things down. Issues mostly evaporate once on the page (in your diary) and it's a lot more effective for rationalizing your emotions than a shouting match across the office. Yes, you now keep a diary – it's made all the difference. It helps you calculate the solutions and realize the opportunities thrown up by the problems. And it's kept a lid on those overly emotional reactions.
4. *Increments.* Your life will improve immeasurably. Yet this won't happen overnight, as you seem to expect. But nor will it happen gradually. It will happen in increments – deliberate steps that, slowly and over time, get you to a better place.

Some – like joining a gym or starting a diary – will be tiny steps, hardly noticeable to the outside world. Others – like starting a business – are major moments that will take planning and some courage. Yet they're all steps taken consciously. And they're all self-reinforcing: meaning their benefits become apparent reasonably quickly and bolster the decision to make the move. That said, nearly always, there'll be a price to pay: money, time, emotions, pride, even relationships. Be prepared to pay it.

5. *Discriminate.* Other than your emotions, your key problem is focus: you lack it. Frustration has led you towards indiscriminate activity in the hope of something working out. Yet the effort soon dissipates, leaving you floundering around for the next 'big push'. Indeed, such poor focus has been one of your worst adult handicaps – leaving you frustrated, bewildered and depressed. Luckily, all that's about to change. You finally generate a desire – for starting a PR agency for the City – that gives you a laser-like focus. This well-honed (and written down) goal improves your judgement and even changes your luck (something you previously thought you lacked).
6. *Realize nothing's perfect.* Such focus also kills another handicap that's so far held you back – waiting for the perfect circumstances in order to act. Perfection, like the white knight, is a myth. Seeking perfectionism is therefore no more than an excuse for procrastination – causing you to miss good (but not perfect) opportunities. This adds regret to your list of negative emotions. Indeed, expecting the perfect circumstances also means you expect perfect outcomes – another impossibility that adds to your sense of regret.
7. *Learn lessons.* As stated, a great deal goes wrong. But, again, the focus helps. Finally, you start learning from the many mistakes that you, indeed, continue to make. In fact, many of the mistakes have been self-inflicted repetitions of previous errors simply because you failed to learn the lesson (instead focusing on shifting the blame). Yet mistakes are fantastic

learning tools. As lessons, they move you on to the next level (a next level full of different potential mistakes, it's worth noting). Unlearnt, however, and – like a computer game – you stay trapped at the lower level.

8. *Cut the party short.* Jeez, you've spent an awful lot of time focused on your social life – getting drunk every weekend and sometimes during the week: all killing productivity far more than you realize. What a waste! Friends are important, of course, but they need to fit around your career – not the other way around. Hedonism has no future, and it's vastly overrated – causing a good percentage of your personal problems. Sorry to cut the party short, but the excess has gotta go – and that includes the classic young man's obsession with sex. Far better to channel all that energy towards more productive pursuits.
9. *Be a fantasist.* If the career you want doesn't materialize – invent one. In fact, that's exactly what you do in the end, although only once you'd turned those ill-formed fantasies into a proper plan – with definite milestones, a strategy and some tactics for execution.
10. *Regret what you do.* Your deepest regrets will be based on what you didn't do, not on what you did. Sure there are things you did you wish you hadn't – but, in time, nearly all of these generate a smile or, at worst, a wry shrug. It's where you failed to act – the roads you didn't take – that the regret eats away at your soul.

## Chaos reigns

In fact, there's an eleventh point, although one too important to share in a list. It's what I say to my team when things go wrong, although – I have to admit – it also undermines the entire premise of this book.

'It's all chaos,' I often declare.

What I mean by this is that, by its very nature, life is uncontrollable. After all, we're just tiny organisms clinging to a speck of rock that's hurtling through space. Of course, we spend our time trying to gain an element of control over our lives – quite rightly. We acquire skills and seek work in order to buy shelter and travel further up Maslow's hierarchy of needs. But the notion of total control – of eradicating any element of our life that's out of control – is impossible.

It's also worth noting that, from the above tips – and perhaps unusually for a book about productivity – none of the recommendations I made to my younger self involved anally retentive information processing, or minute-by-minute time strictures. Quite the opposite. Your focus should be on setting a broad outline for your life, before creating some sort of sequential order, based on your best guess at the practical steps required for execution. And then get going as best you can.

Anything too inflexible will snap. As stated in Part One, sustained motivation is the key – helped by concepts such as finding 'flow'. Yet my guess is that flow will arrive when you discover something you love, which is usually something you're good at. Once you find flow, motivation will then be largely due to structure, which means developing a critical path for execution. Of course, success (or at least progress) will keep you motivated, which is great. But you'll also need to calculate how to overcome the occasional obstacle.

And the rest is mere detail. In fact it's chaos – from which you have to snatch the elements you need for your progress.

## The joy of winging it

I'll end on a personal note. My PR firm has just turned ten years' old. This means I've spent a decade nurturing a company from the ground up. In fact – given that I had zero experience in public relations when I created the company (just an idea for producing 'expertise based' PR) – the concept of 'starting' a business was quite literally true in my case. I had to learn the strategies and tactics that are the stock-in-trade of PR executives. And I had to make every lesson count, no matter how embarrassing the mistake.

Those early days were an extraordinary mix of confusion, excitement, anticipation and suppressed panic: I loved it, but it also terrified me. I felt a great sense of freedom – that anything was possible – but also an underlying sense of dread. Surely, someone would point out that I couldn't do this? That I was simply making it up as I went along. That I was an amateur, a chancer, an imposter: and that I was 'winging it' to an audience that would eventually work me out and slam the door.

In fact, I *was* a chancer. And an imposter. And I was, pretty much, making it up as I went along. That said, I'd done my research and – at the very least – knew that my target audience was being poorly served by the existing PR offering. There was a classic gap in the market, even if I'd still to establish how, exactly, I could fill that gap.

So what's my point? Two really. That we can move forward with imperfect knowledge – in fact we must, because perfect knowledge is impossible. And that the chaos doesn't subside as the journey progresses: at least not if we want to keep moving forward.

Hence my phrase 'it's all chaos' regularly stated to sometimes panicked colleagues in the office – usually after some minor disaster has unfolded that they're (mistakenly) looking for me to solve.

Quite rightly, they plan a particular campaign meticulously – down to the meetings scheduled and the phone calls required: where, when and with whom. They have sheets of instructions, lists, press releases, FAQs and Q&As – all pre-prepared and pre-approved. And then they execute, which results in every last element of their highly calculated plan going straight out the window.

'No plan survives contact with the enemy', said Helmuth von Moltke, the renowned German general, although what he meant by this wasn't that the goal should change or our objectives be in anyway compromised. It's that – having established the strategy and tactics for a particular pursuit – they'll act as a strong benchmark for our actions: no more.

We have a plan – great! But it's almost certainly wrong in ways we've yet to discover. Indeed, it's wrong in ways that only execution can reveal – the 'unknown unknowns' of Defense Secretary Donald Rumsfeld's famous phrase during the Iraq War.

Does this make planning pointless? Absolutely not. To use one last military quote, 'plans are nothing, planning is everything'. This one's from General Dwight D. Eisenhower who, like von Moltke, was simply stating that any action involves countless twists and turns that cannot possibly be predicted. But we must plan for it anyway.

So we can plan for a positive outcome, but – once we've started to execute – we can guarantee something will turn up that knocks us slightly off course, which makes knowing the course (towards our goal) all the more important. Meanwhile plans without flexibility – with no give – are asking to be rendered useless almost immediately.

And this explains the 'all is chaos' comment to my team. They need the confidence to act, which planning gives them. But they also need the confidence to keep acting once their plans prove inadequate, as they will.

They've done nothing wrong – quite the opposite. They've fired up the machine, and some of the atoms have gone off in unexpected directions. Fine: let's stay on top of it, re-evaluate as we proceed and keep going – using all that planning as a good basis for further planning.

In my view, this is the single most important lesson anyone can learn. There are no perfect circumstances for taking action. There are no perfect outcomes. Compromise is a certainty. If we therefore spend our lives trying to create the perfect circumstances, or perfect outcome – or if we avoid the cost or refuse the compromise – we'll spend our lives in frustrated paralysis.

## Act or be acted upon

But there's another important point here. The result of inaction isn't neutral. The score doesn't remain at zero, or nil-nil. In fact it rapidly becomes minus 100. Why? Because, if we refuse to act on our own account, we'll find ourselves no more than the pawns of those who are taking action towards *their* own goals.

'Act or be acted upon', said Stephen Covey (1989) – meaning we're either in charge of our own progress (imperfect as that progress may be) or we'll be recruited by someone else in order to assist *their* progress.

Indeed, there's no alternative to these two choices. If we opt out – perhaps becoming a hippy – fine, we're still making an active choice with its own objectives, strategic requirements and endeavours. If we cannot muster even that obtuse – but legitimate – goal, then we'll almost certainly find ourselves the unwilling recruit of more motivated people: even if they're people we never meet such as political ideologues, Latin-American drug lords or daytime TV schedulers.

So, we have a choice. Make plans and take positive action – no matter what the pursuit or how offensive the goal to our significant others. Or we can do nothing and let others control our destiny, which will almost certainly, somewhere along the line, be unplanned and unpleasant.

## Are you ready?

Ending on an admonishment will win me few friends, however – not least because it's both unnecessary and ineffective. Too many people lectured me in my youth – about my disabling self-beliefs, about my directionless even feckless pursuits, about my self-fulfilling self-hatred – without it making any difference. In fact, the impact was negative: compounding my funk, exacerbating my sense of isolation, exaggerating the dread. Yet that's because I wasn't ready to listen.

In Part One I mentioned the friend who snapped at my ineffective negativity and, finally, shook me from my self-absorbed and negative stupor. Yet his was a lecture I'd heard many times before, but ignored. He got through because it was what I needed to hear at that moment. I was ready. This leaves you to ponder whether the time is right for you to listen to that message also. And, if you've managed to keep reading to this point, then I think the answer's obvious.

**Get Things Done:** *Chaos reigns, so we need to become comfortable with the fact there are limits to what we can control. Plans will and must be altered during execution, although the objectives should remain set. That said, there are no perfect circumstances, or results: we just need to act.*

# THE 7 HABITS OF HIGHLY *INEFFECTIVE* PEOPLE

Stephen Covey's famous work (*7 Habits of Highly Effective People*) is probably the most influential self-help book ever written. That said, his book makes the same mistake as many others: an assumption that we're pure potential – a malleable blob capable of absorbing effective and sustainable habits once we're made aware of them.

If only it were so.

Too often we're anything but malleable. We're not raw material waiting to be shaped, but damaged goods: poorly-programmed or misshapen machines condemned by our ineffective behaviour and deeply-ingrained negative habits.

Below, and from bitter experience, I outline what I see as the seven worst habits (though there may be plenty more) of highly *ineffective* people: sometimes – but not always – mirroring Covey's own. And, in each case, it's also worth noting the more positive alternative.

## 1. Procrastination

There's been plenty written on procrastination already, although describing it as a habit truly puts it in its place. Strip away the psychology, and procrastination is no more than repeated ineffective behaviour. It's inaction despite numerous prompts and impulses – a habitual resistance no matter how aware we are of the need for action.

Indeed, Covey implores us to 'act'. His first habit is to 'be proactive' – expressing the gap between those that act and those that don't as the 'difference between night and day'. Yet he misses the fact that inaction is not a neutral state. It's not a car waiting for the engine to start. It's more a broken-down vehicle being pushed uphill – meaning we'll simply roll back to the bottom the second the pressure's relaxed.

Only the motivation that comes from strong planning can break this poor habit: willpower is not enough.

## 2. Avoiding direction

A key reason we procrastinate is our lack of direction. Without direction we're going nowhere, meaning that even action will simply send us round in circles. In fact, without direction, action is no more than inaction in disguise.

And being directionless is a habit because it resists any attempt at future thinking. Life is something that just happens to the directionless, a notion that can quickly become ingrained. In fact it can feel and sound positive – that we're 'laid back' perhaps, or that we 'take life as it comes'.

Yet this is the curse of being 'cool', in my opinion: a habit where the short-term results exact a heavy long-term price.

Only strong planning can break such a habitual cycle. And that requires long-term goals that inspire us to the point we're motivated to not only take action (that's the easy bit) but to meticulously research and plan the required strategies and tactics, including their sequence.

## 3. Blaming others

Why do we avoid planning? The single most common reason is our inner belief that someone will come to our rescue. Worse, this can involve someone we perceive 'owes us'. Too often, we blame others for our poor fate – usually those we think have harmed us (parents, siblings, those in authority, or even 'the rich').

Yet blame is an appallingly ineffectual habit because we've simply outsourced our future to the very people least likely to help us. Expecting a sibling or parent or our boss to have a major mental conversion and dedicate their lives to making amends is a ridiculously self-harming belief and one likely to make us both ineffective and miserable.

The absolute beginning for those wanting to replace poor habits with strong ones, therefore, is to realize it's our responsibility to do so. It's crazy to wait for someone else to help us: not least because – even if they do – they've simply further reduced our autonomy.

## 4. Obsessing about others' impact on us

Those with low autonomy often share a habit that disables their ability to utilize an important tool: other people. They're 100 percent focused on the impact others have on them – an obsession that wrecks their effectiveness.

Indeed, even cursory encounters can disable our progress if we're only observing their impact on us. Disinterested shop assistants for instance, or a close friend or potential employer perhaps 'disrespecting' us: indeed, any interaction can obsess us to the point we search their responses for signs that support our negative self-beliefs.

Of course, this surrenders our ability to shape events in our favour. We're now reliant on them – even for compliments and encouragement: a habit potentially so ingrained that we strip ourselves of *any* autonomy.

Get direction, however, and our concerns regarding others' impact on us is reversed. It's now our goals that matter: not our immediate needs regarding how we're being perceived or treated.

With a plan, that shop assistant is no more than someone furnishing a required instrument for our progress (perhaps some smart shoes), which makes their treatment of us irrelevant.

Indeed, if we turn the table – and focus on our impact on them – we can become highly effective when dealing with people. Pay compliments, for instance, and power will flow from our words: putting us in charge of *any* encounter, which can then be measured purely on the basis of whether we've managed to make progress towards our goals, or not.

## 5. Having a fixed mindset

Connected with this is Carol Dweck's excellent notion (from her 2006 book *Mindset*) that the world divides into those with a 'fixed' – and those with a 'growth' – mindset. Having a fixed mindset is an ineffectual habit in the extreme as it assumes our attributes, and even our knowledge, is fixed. Our skills are innate, which means we spend our lives proving to others our worth, or – more likely – hiding our self-perceived lack of worth.

Yet this poor habit is easily reversed. We simply need to adopt a growth mindset, in which we acknowledge we have 'everything to learn'. We therefore see all situations or encounters as opportunities to acquire knowledge or skills, which is far more effective than trying to showcase our (perhaps limited) fixed attributes.

A growth mindset not only means we're open to learning, which is more effective than wasting time trying to prove our status to others. It also gives off positive vibes: that we're interested in what others have to offer, which does wonders for their view of us – a highly effective habit indeed.

## 6. Ignoring progress

When all's said and done, we can make progress anyway, despite our poor habits. But if we fail to notice our advances – perhaps by retaining our negative self-beliefs – we'll remain mentally trapped: still railing against our poor luck or blaming others despite our elevated position. Any promotion will simply open doors to new levels of insecurity – new avenues for blame and fear.

And a key part of this is the fact we've failed to record the progress we make, which makes any advances feel random and therefore unsustainable. Indeed, our advances may only become apparent in their loss, something we may have viewed as inevitable given our poor self-beliefs.

This is classic territory for the ineffective. Yet, just as our poor fortune is our own concern, so is our good fortune. We must note our progress, however slow. And the best way to do this is by keeping a daily diary: one that heeds the teachings from both setbacks and, even more importantly, understands the why and wherefore of our advances, which makes any progress both satisfying and replicable.

## 7. Being derailed by every setback

This is one of my worst habits – being sent right back to square one by even the smallest setback. If every setback is treated as confirmation that we're a 'bad person', then we're unlikely to make sustainable progress. In fact, progress feels like a lie because, inwardly, we still feel incapable. This makes our successes no more than 'luck', which – given our poor self-beliefs – will certainly generate the inevitable reckoning of the permanently 'unlucky'.

Yet setbacks are an inevitable part of any journey. In fact, they can even be welcomed as strong benchmarks for attainment – allowing us to know what works, because we can so clearly see what hasn't worked.

For the ineffective, however, setbacks are a total derailment. And such derailments have become a habit, meaning we look for derailment: even manufacturing the circumstances for derailment if none are readily available.

Meanwhile, those with effective habits see derailment as one result, no more. It may mean they're doing something in the wrong way or that they need somehow to hone a skill or acquire new information.

And it's worth noting that both reactions are a choice. The facts remain the same – it's the interpretation that's wildly different. So we may as well choose the reaction that helps our progress.

# BIBLIOGRAPHY


Allen, David (2001) *Getting Things Done*, London: Piatkus.

Bazerman, Max H. (2005) *Judgement in Managerial Decision Making*, Hoboken, N.J: John Wiley & Sons.

Burka, Jane B. & Yuen, Lenora M. (1983) *Procrastination*, Cambridge, MA: Da Capo Press.

Blumenthal, Noah (2007) *You're Addicted to You*, San Francisco: Berrett-Koehler.

Carlson, Richard (1998) *Don't Sweat the Small Stuff at Work*, London: Hyperion.

Carnegie, Dale (1936) *How to Win Friends and Influence People*, New York: Simon & Schuster.

Caunt, John (2002) *Boost Your Self Esteem*, London: Kogan Page.

Covey, Stephen (1989) *Seven Habits of Highly Effective People*, New York: Simon & Schuster.

Cook, Marshall (1999) *Streetwise Time Management*, Avon, MA: Adams Media.

Dweck, Carol (2007) *Mindset*, New York: Ballantine Books.

Duhigg, Charles (2012) *The Power of Habits*, London: William Heinemann.

Evans, Sybil (2000) *Hot Buttons*, London: Piatkus.

Festinger, Leon (1957) *A Theory of Cognitive Dissonance*, Stanford, CA: Stanford University Press.

Frankl, Viktor (1959) *Man's Search For Meaning*, London: Ebury Publishing.

Freud, Sigmund (1923/2001) *The Ego and the Id and Other Works* Vol.19 in The Complete Psychological Works of Sigmund Freud, London: Vintage Classics.

Friedman, Stewart D. & Greenhaus, Jeffrey H. (2000) *Work and Family – Allies or Enemies*, Oxford: Oxford University Press.

Goleman, Daniel (1995) *Emotional Intelligence*, London: Bloomsbury.

Goleman, Daniel (1998) *Working with Emotional Intelligence*, London: Bloomsbury.

Gorman, Tom (2007) *Motivation*, Edina, MN: Adams Business.

Gray, John (1992) *Men Are From Mars, Women Are From Venus*, London: HarperCollins.

Greene, Robert (2000) *The 48 Laws of Power*, London: Profile Books.

Griessman, B. Eugene (1994) *Time Tactics of Very Successful People*, New York: McGraw-Hill.

Hartmann, Thomas (1998) *Healing ADD*, Grass Valley, CA: Underwood Books.

Harvard Business Essential (2006) *Decision Making*, Cambridge, MA: Harvard Business School Press.

Hawkins, Charlie (2008) *Make Meetings Matter*, Pompton Plains, NJ: Career Press.

Heppell, Michael (2011) *How to Save an Hour Every Day*, Harlow: Prentice Hall.

Hoch, Stephen J. & Kunreuther, C. Howard (2001) *Wharton on Making Decisions*, Hoboken N.J: John Wiley & Sons.

Hill, Napoleon (1937/2007) *Think and Grow Rich*, Hoboken NJ: Capstone.

Hill, Napoleon (1928/2007) *Law of Success*, Thousand Oaks, CA: BN Publishing.

James, Oliver (2002) *They F*** You Up*, London: Bloomsbury.

Kerzner, Harold (2006) *Project Management*, Hoboken N.J: John Wiley & Sons.

Koch, Richard (2005) *Living the 80/20 Way*, Boston, MA: Nicholas Brealey.

Krznaric, Roman (2012) *How to Find Fulfilling Work*, London: MacMillan.

Lafair, Sylvia (2009) *Don't Bring it to Work*, Hoboken, NJ. John Wiley & Sons.

Lakhani, Dave (2005) *Persuasion: the Art of Getting What You Want*, Hoboken, NJ: John Wiley & Sons.

Luecke, Richard A. & McIntosh, Perry (2009) *The Busy Manager's Guide to Delegation*, New York: AMACOM.

Mackenzie, Alec (1972) *The Time Trap*, New York: AMACOM.

McCormack, Mark H (1984/2003) *What They Don't Teach You at Harvard Business School*, London: Profile Books.

McIntosh, Perry & Luecke, Richard A (2010) *Increase Your Influence at Work*, New York: AMACOM.

McKay, Matthew, & Fanning, Patrick (2000) *Self-Esteem*, Oakland, CA: New Harbinger Publications.

Maslow, Abraham (1943) *A Theory of Human Motivation*, Washington DC: *Psychological Review* (journal).

Machiavelli, Niccolò (2003) *The Prince*, Oxford: Oxford University Press, 1513/2008.

Maté, Gabor (2000) *Scattered*, New York: Plume Books.

Morgenstern, Julie (2004) *Organizing From The Inside Out*, London: Hodder & Stoughton.

Morgenstern, Julie (2005) *Never Check Email in the Morning*, Whitby, ON: Fireside.

Morgenstern, Julie (2008) *When Organizing Isn't Enough*, Whitby, ON: Fireside.

Nelson, Mike (2001) *Stop Clutter From Stealing Your Life*, Pompton Plains, NJ: New Page Books.

Orman, Suze (2003) *The Laws of Money, the Lessons of Life*. New York: Simon & Schuster.

Paul, Dr Marilyn (2009) *Why Am I So Disorganised?* London: Piatkus.

Paul, Richard W & Elder, Linda (2003) *Critical Thinking*, Harlow, UK: Prentice Hall.

Pearson, Pat (2008) *Stop Self-Sabotage*, New York: McGraw-Hill.

Plous, Scott (1993) *The Psychology of Judgement and Decision Making*, New York: McGraw Hill.

Robbins, Anthony (1987) *Unlimited Power*, London: Simon & Schuster.

Roesch, Roberta (1998) *Time Management for Busy People*, New York: McGraw Hill.

Satir, Virginia (1988) *The New Peoplemaking*, Palo Alto, CA: Science and Behaviour Books.

Sudderth, David B., & Kandel, Joseph (1996) *Adult ADD – The Complete Handbook*, New York: Three Rivers Press.

Sun-Tsu (translated by Sawyer, Ralph D.) (2005) *Art of War*, New York: Basic Books.

Tracy, Brian (2004) *Eat That Frog*, London: Hodder Headline.

Tracy, Brian (2003) *Goals!* San Francisco: Berrett-Koehler.

Tracy, Brian (1993) *Maximum Achievement*, New York: Simon & Schuster.

Ursiny, Tim (2003) *The Coward's Guide to Conflict*, Naperville, IL: Sourcebooks.

# ABOUT ROBERT KELSEY

In 2011 the Capstone imprint of John Wiley & Sons, Ltd published *What's Stopping You?*, a book exploring why smart people often fail to reach their potential. This was Robert Kelsey's first successful book after what he perceived as the failure of his debut book, a lad-lit comedy detailing his life as a British investment banker in New York. Indeed, that book – *The Pursuit of Happiness* – was written to explain Robert's perceived failure as a banker: one selling highly toxic financial products to the likes of Enron.

Notice the word 'perceived' in the above descriptions. In both cases it was Robert's self-beliefs that condemned his pursuits as failures – resulting in actions that, indeed, confirmed that status.

Yet the link between these career disasters and the success of *What's Stopping You?* is Robert's noble attempt to research and explain his own insecurities. This is a personal journey – one in which he concluded that behind every career and academic disaster, as well as every seemingly unsustainable success, lay his deep lack of confidence. He also realized that his early-life experiences were trapping him in a cycle of low self-esteem – generating either low-attainment (further knocking his confidence) or modest attainment (resulting in hubris and near-certain disaster).

*Get Things Done* is the third of Robert's series of books looking into his personal history, and the psychology and early-life conditioning that created such an ineffective young adult. Oddly, of the mental barriers to his own success, he realized this is the easiest to overcome: once motivated to do so, and once able to adopt the rather simple traits and attributes of highly effective people. While fear of failure is an innate condition we must learn to accept and navigate, and confidence an alchemy we can create only once we learn to discriminate, Robert's view is that getting things done is little more than a process involving the generation of plans and the adoption of habits based on our desires. Motivation is the key, and it's here where Kelsey starts his journey towards redemption – once he's slain a few myths regarding the causes of poor productivity.

Robert runs a financial PR agency in the City of London and lives with his wife and two boys in London and Suffolk. Having overcome his phobia of public speaking, he also gives the occasional talk.

# INDEX

Printed and bound by CPI Group (UK) Ltd, Croydon, CR0 4YY

22/05/2025

14675027-0001